# VASTLY MORE THAN THAT

# VASTLY MORE THAN THAT

## STORIES OF LESBIANS & GAY MEN IN RECOVERY

## GUY KETTELHACK

HAZELDEN®

INFORMATION & EDUCATIONAL SERVICES

Hazelden
Center City, Minnesota 55012-0176

1-800-328-0094
1-651-213-4590 (Fax)
www.hazelden.org

**Library of Congress Cataloging-in-Publication Data**
Kettelhack, Guy.
      Vastly more than that : stories of lesbians and gay men in
  recovery / Guy Kettelhack.
          p.   cm.
      ISBN 1-56838-205-7
      1. Gays—Alcohol use—United States.   2. Gays—Substance use—
United States.   3. Alcoholics—Rehabilitation—United States.
4. Addicts—Rehabilitation—United States.    5. Recovering addicts—
United States.   6. Compulsive behavior—United States.    I. Title.
HV5139.K48  1999
362.292'086'64—dc21                          98-49510
                                                     CIP

*Editor's note*

All the stories in this book are based on actual experiences. The names and
details have been changed to protect the privacy of the people involved. In
some cases, composites have been created.

03 02 01 00 99  6 5 4 3 2

Cover design by Theresa Gedig
Interior design by Donna Burch
Typesetting by Stanton Publication Services, Inc.

*to Gordon Thomas,*
*for the title,*

*Steve Lehman,*
*for his editing*

*and Dan Odegard,*
*for his vision*

He cannot picture life without alcohol. Some day he will be unable to imagine life either with alcohol or without it. Then he will know loneliness such as few do. He will be at the jumping-off place. He will wish for the end.

We have shown how we got out from under. You say, "Yes, I'm willing. But am I to be consigned to a life where I shall be stupid, boring and glum, like some righteous people I see? I know I must get along without liquor, but how can I? Have you a sufficient substitute?"

Yes, there is a substitute and it is vastly more than that.

—*Alcoholics Anonymous*, third edition
The "Big Book"

# Contents

# Acknowledgments

I am deeply grateful to David Groff for having lent me the idea for this book, to Gordon Eugene Thomas whose bright and beautiful mind saw what the book could be, gave it its current title, and ran with it—ran with it to the extraordinary editorial team at Hazelden: Dan Odegard and Steve Lehman who embraced the book and some-how—Steve, especially, who was my on-the-page editor—tolerated all of the delays and anguish and boulders of resistance I proceeded to put in front of myself before I could actually write the damned thing. These people are "clueless" in the best possible sense of the word: open and receptive and trusting and remarkably able to wed heart to mind in a business whose operating motive usually has to do with a very different kind of bottom line. They richly deserve the dedication they've received in this book.

I am indebted beyond the capacity to express it to the legions of lesbians and gay men who've kept me sober and whose stories have inspired this book, as well as to the following people: Peter Hammond, Donna Boguslav, and Richard Bell, who still reside on the planet; and Reuven Closter, Joseph Velez, and Connie Clausen, who, to my eternal and unspeakable sorrow, no longer do.

# 1 There's More in Your Sandbox Than You Think

One summer day in 1989, at the end of a daily early morning AA meeting at which we both were regulars, Philip asked me to be his sponsor. I froze. By the time of his request I had nearly four years of sobriety, four often rewarding, often bewildering years of learning how to exist without the soporific "help" of upwards of two quarts of vodka a day—the amount I was drinking by the moment, about 3 A.M. on an October morning in 1985, I was battered into the epiphany not only that I couldn't bear the hell my life had become, but that vodka was the main reason it had become hell. (That I'd narrowly missed being knifed by a teenaged kid I tried to pay to have sex with me helped to punctuate the point.) But four years, however hard won, didn't seem nearly enough sobriety to handle someone like Philip.

Philip was a formidable presence: he'd had almost a year of tumultuous sobriety himself—a year nearly every tortured second of which he chronicled for us, morning after morning, often straining my patience and, I suspect, the patience of most of the rest of the recovering alcoholics to whom he subjected his every last smoldering resentment. Sobriety seemed to be as great a hell to Philip as his drinking life had ever been. Angry and imperious and impatient, Philip clearly was not going to take no for an answer: asking me to be his sponsor sounded more like a command than a request.

Philip was born Felipe, the son of a Puerto Rican, heavy-drinking, obese earth mother who had been on welfare nearly all of her son's life, and a Venezuelan middle-class father who remarried shortly after leaving Philip's mother (when Felipe was not quite two) and had since engendered a whole new brood, a horde of stepbrothers and stepsisters whom Philip barely knew and didn't want to know. Philip's father was a successful businessman, a man who had managed to exploit his adopted country's economic system much more successfully than, or at least very differently from, Philip's mother. Anglicizing his name from Felipe to Philip was his father's idea: "If you want to succeed in this country, you have to play the game," and, if you were Latino, part of playing the game clearly meant underplaying your ethnic background.

It was clear from Philip's angry morning meeting outbursts that he waged love/hate affairs with both his parents, alternately railing against his mother (with whom he not only lived, but shared a bed) for her drunken negligence and laziness and praising her "let it all hang out" acceptance of life-as-it-happened; alternately cursing his father for selling out and pretending to be a *gringo* and praising him for making money and becoming a respectable man with a big house and productive family in suburban New Jersey. It was unclear whether or not Philip's father and mother had ever been married (Philip's surname was different from his mother's, which perplexed me, since I knew she'd never remarried), but his father had demonstrated a responsible streak by putting Philip through a Roman Catholic boarding school and sending him to a big, well-known Catholic university in the Midwest. Philip's childhood and adolescence thus were a confusing, divisive mix of Irish Catholic nuns and blond, blue-eyed Irish Catholic boys who branded Philip dismissively as "Latino street kid" and long hot summer days sitting on stoops of his mother's family's rent-controlled tenement homes on the Lower East Side of Manhattan, drinking wine and beer and eating deep-fried plantains and pork cracklings (becoming, as a consequence, as fat as his mother), eyed with suspicion by his Puerto Rican relatives as "uppity"—trying to seem better than they were because he was college-bound and could talk like an educated white person. Philip/Felipe was never sure which side of the family he was supposed to emulate: he was never sure who he was supposed to be.

The fact that Philip was gay was another monkey wrench in his torn life, another reason to feel different not only from both sides of his determinedly heterosexual family, but also from most of the Irish Catholic white kids with whom he associated during the school year. However, he never mentioned anything about his sexuality in his sharing at the morning meeting; as detailed as his angry tirades against his mother and father and neighbors and coffee-shop waiters and Laundromat attendants and landlord were, you always had the sense that something central, something far more pressing and volatile and unbearable, was being withheld: Philip's rage had some source that you knew he hadn't yet named.

And yet he stayed sober. And he went to this meeting every morning. And sometimes—albeit rarely—a softer, more receptive self would emerge: a funnier, more tolerant Philip, a slightly stunned, childlike version. Sometimes other people's pain would reach him, and when it came his time to speak (our morning meeting was organized as "round-robin," enabling a lot of shy people who would otherwise have stayed silent to share), he would then be uncharacteristically hesitant and tender—able, for a brief moment, to reveal something more ambiguous and confused and open-ended in his nature, a sweetness he otherwise never allowed us to see.

What I had not realized was that Philip had been studying me and that his rare moments of "sweetness" were often triggered by hearing my own urgent outpourings, bursts of anger and sorrow especially engendered by the recent death of my brother from AIDS. I can't remember everything I spilled out about this, but I know I held back very little about what it was like to fly out to L.A. and take care of my dying older brother, cleaning him up, calming him down during his protracted hysterical spates of dementia, and finally watching him die. It turned out that Philip hadn't missed a nuance of this experience, and it was because of what he saw me go through, and how he saw me go through it, that he asked me to be his sponsor. But I didn't know this when he asked me to sponsor him. I said yes almost because I was afraid to say no. As I expect I've now made clear, Philip wasn't someone whose requests you could easily deny.

Thus began a relationship sometimes as stormy and torn as any Philip or I had had in either of our lives with any lover or family member or friend, before or after sobriety. Philip was a big man, overweight, over six feet, topping 260 pounds, and a couple of years older than I. I've waned and waxed weightwise in sobriety (sometimes seeking in Dunkin' Donuts the relief and escape I used to find in vodka), but I always felt like a little mouse next to an elephant when I was with Philip. Something about his commanding size and style made the sponsor-sponsee relationship we were supposed to be having seem a little absurd, at least if you subscribed to the notion that "sponsor" was supposed to know a hell of a lot more about sober life than "sponsee." Philip was not the type to take "suggestions" from anybody, and the more I got to know him, the fewer suggestions I felt capable of making to him. Mostly what I did was listen when he spoke, which, over time, proved more often than not to be the right tack to take—not only for him, but for me.

About six months into our largely one-sided relationship (he talked, I listened), during one of our weekly postmeeting breakfasts at an East Village Ukrainian coffee shop, Philip revealed the reason he'd chosen me as his sponsor. "I'm HIV positive," he said, "and I figured that if you could bear taking care of your brother, cleaning up his messes, being there even when it got as bad as it got, well, maybe you'd take care of me—when the time came." If I'd frozen when he'd first asked me to be his sponsor, this confession turned me into a glacier. Philip had singled me out to see him through AIDS, to be there when he died, to do for him what he'd heard me say I'd done for my brother. I nearly choked on my coffee. There was no way I wanted to go through anything like that again, especially not with someone—well, someone like Philip. The dark secret was, I wasn't sure I even *liked* Philip all that much. Truth be told, I was submitting to our sponsor-sponsee agreement out of a sense of obligation, out of some dimly felt requirement that you shouldn't say no to another suffering alcoholic, even if you'd rather crawl into a dark hole, take the phone off the hook, and eat doughnuts.

But because Philip was in good health—he hadn't evinced any opportunistic infection so far—we both could retreat into at least a partial feeling that getting sick or dying from AIDS had no reality: maybe Philip would simply turn out to be one of those HIV-positive gay men who just never got sick. Experts at denial, we happily subscribed to this notion, and I went back to listening, he to talking. Those years—there were four of them— were pivotal ones in both our lives. Philip watched me squirm uneasily out of a twelve-and-a-half-year relationship with a man who'd put up with me when I was a drunk *and* lived with me sober, but from whom I now felt I had to detach myself to construct (for the first time) a solo life, a life where *my* name was on the lease, on the utility bill, in the phone book. Philip watched me—at the age of forty—struggle to achieve some kind of unprecedented autonomy, learning in sobriety how to take care of myself and how to live alone for the first time in my life. And Philip followed my example. He'd been living with his mother in a tiny one-bedroom East Village apartment, letting nobody but me know that he slept in the same bed with her, owing mostly to the fact that there was no other place *but* that bed for him to sleep. Then his mother had a stroke. Philip was galvanized into action. Long an expert at playing the New York City welfare system like a virtuoso on the violin, Philip managed not only to get his mother quite astonishingly expert (and free) medical care but also to set her up in her own apartment farther down on the Lower East Side, cared for on three eight-hour shifts (that is, twenty-four hours a day) by various Puerto Rican nurse attendants—his mother could speak no English despite having lived in New York City for nearly fifty years—whose daily ministrations he monitored like a hawk. He turned their once shared apartment into his own royal abode, repainting the kitchen cabinets, buying a new mattress for the bed, and otherwise reclaiming his mother's space as his own. If I were going to get my own home, he would get his own home too.

And oh, the Walter Mitty fantasies he shared with me! Lord (finally) of his own manor, he made it clear that this was only the first of many much grander homes he would one day inhabit: first, of course, he'd make his way as a painter (he'd majored in art in college), taking the New York art world by storm; then he'd find a roomy one-bedroom in a brand-new Trump-owned glossy highrise, one sunny northern-exposed corner of which he would turn into his studio, the whole effect of the place metallic and silver and white, stripped to essentials, a perfect spread for *Architectural Digest*. Of course, ultimately he'd find a small cottage near the beach on the Jersey shore (his father regularly took his current crop of kids there for summer vacations), where he'd live year-round, inviting other noteworthy artists for weekends during which they'd share tricks of the trade and at which they'd all marvel at his latest trendsetting work—collages in tasteful taupes, ecrus, and faint purples and blues, which would inspire a kind of mystical reverie in anyone who gazed on them. And, it went without saying, there'd be a perfect lover—not some "vanilla" lovey-dovey white boy, but someone with an edge—someone who'd explore the kinkier side of things with Philip. (By now he'd given me some quite lurid accounts of past orgies at the baths and at clubs like The Mineshaft. Philip had been quite an aficionado of New York's many sex venues in the mid-1970s.)

His daily life was taken up in more vengeful fantasy, some of which he quite effectively acted out. A neighbor's air conditioner made too much noise, so Philip sent registered letters to his landlord with official-sounding complaints (the texts of which I've still got in my computer; he'd asked me to type them out, making sure the margins on each of his threatening letters were even—top, bottom, and sides; Philip would allow nothing he committed to writing to be less than a work of art), copies of which he'd send to various New York City bureaucratic offices, his councilman, and his senator. He nearly got that neighbor evicted, and he certainly succeeded in getting him to turn off his air conditioner after nine o'clock at night. And, as I've said, he was an amazing caretaker for his stricken mother: the New York City welfare bureaucrats were not accustomed to someone as smart and relentless as Philip, and he managed to create an extraordinary life of luxury for her—for free.

But most of Philip's fantasies remained fantasies. When one belligerent drunken neighbor regularly came home late, slamming the front door of the building, waking Philip up, Philip

began investigating martial arts and boxing gyms, planning to become a vicious no-holds-barred fighter who would leap on this un-
suspecting drunk the next time he dared to make noise at two
o'clock in the morning. (This decision soon passed on its own with
no further comment from either of us.) Long fascinated by various
decks of tarot cards, and with a late-sixties/early-seventies history
of pot smoking, taking LSD, and joining a mystical brotherhood
in Portland, Oregon, where he'd lived for several years after college, Philip confided to me his decision ultimately to open up a
spiritual (drug-free) school in which he'd instruct people in amal-
gams of various arcane arts, an all-embracing system derived
equally from cabalistic mysticism and the powerful magic of
Caribbean voodoo, which he'd sometimes attempt (unsuccess-
fully) to explain to me by means of various intricate mandalas he
had meticulously filled in with brilliant colored pencil.

My own stabs at self-expression prodded him into action as
well: when I sang "Something's Comin'" in a Cherry Grove–Fire
Island summer musical revue and played violin in a comedy skit
in the same show, he decided (after watching the videotape of my
performances, which he quietly admitted gave him goose bumps)
to take voice lessons himself at one of Manhattan's (then numerous, now mostly defunct) support groups for HIV-positive gay
men and announced his plans to find a viola, which he'd teach
himself to play. (He made it clear that the violin was all very nice
but, well, a *bit* high and screechy, didn't I think? He much pre-
ferred the deeper, more mysterious tones of the viola, which he
assured me he would learn quickly and on which he would be
happy, if I wished, to play duets with me at some future time.)

Philip's imagination was wild and brilliant, and the more he
shared its multicolored vagaries with me, the more I marveled at
the richness of his inner world. I do not mean to make him sound

pathetic: the fact that much in these dreams evokes Walter Mitty does not take away from their force and beauty to me. I felt honored to hear them and realize now that he let me know these dreams because I never once made fun of them or in any way implied that they could not be achieved. I'd seen how he'd wrestled the New York welfare system into obeisance; who knew that he couldn't become a mystical, viola-playing, successful painter with an entourage of adoring groupies sitting at his feet in his beachside atelier on the Jersey shore?

Then he began to get sick, which was about the time our relationship began to get stormy. The AIDS virus he harbored soon—maybe two and a half years after we hooked up as sponsor and sponsee—began to cause dementia. Philip grew hazy, dizzy, and unable to remember, sometimes, where he was going or what he had to do. He began sticking up Post-it Notes all over his apartment with names and times and dates, which made his little apartment look like it had been taken over by a flurry of strange yellow butterflies. He began getting angry at me when I didn't return his phone calls instantly or when I brought him the wrong brand of frozen waffles or diet soda. Didn't I realize what he was going through, that he needed me now more than ever? Didn't I realize he was losing his mind? His terror of this slowly overshadowed all else: any mistake of memory not only on his part, but also on my or anyone else's part, felt intolerable to him.

Early on, when the dementia was still sporadic and somewhat manageable, he called together various members of both sides of his family to meet with me and him and his social worker to make tentative plans to care for him. He made it clear that since he did not have a lover, he had chosen me to be the overseer for this care, sharing the responsibility with his uncle (his father's brother), a responsibility that panicked me. I was struck by the intelligence of these family members and the loving attention they gave him but felt profoundly uneasy about the central role Philip wanted me to perform. However, in the days and weeks following this meeting, while he called me at odd hours of the day and night to come over and pick up sandwiches for him at the deli or to return or retrieve a VCR tape (he had a fondness for particularly gory horror movies) from his local video rental store, railing at me (as I've said) for the mistakes I made in choosing the wrong title or brand of whatever it was he wanted, he also managed to engage AIDS caregivers from various city organizations who helped him with the more nitty-gritty aspects of his existence—monitoring his medications, getting him to and from doctors' appointments, and finally getting him into the hospital when it was clear that he couldn't take care of himself at all, alone at home. He made these helpers' lives hell, but they seemed immune to his anger, or maybe simply used to it from the work they'd done with other terrified persons with AIDS. I think Philip knew, deep down, that I wasn't going to be the dream stand-in for a lover he'd hoped I'd be. His instinct for pragmatism had, as always, taken over and saved him: he enlisted the help of people he knew would come through for him, and, at the end, I wasn't one of them.

I remember my last call from Philip, which he logged onto my answering machine: he repeated what he thought was his phone number, to make sure I'd call him back, but the number he gave was the number he'd just dialed—my own.

I didn't return the call.

I knew that by now people he trusted were taking care of him, and my help wasn't "technically" needed. But really I chickened out. I couldn't bear watching him die. I couldn't go through another wasting death from AIDS. Several months later I received a call from one of his mother's relatives, a woman who could barely speak English but who had found my name and number on one of Philip's endless lists. She managed to convey to me that he had died two weeks before, peacefully, in his hospital bed and was buried somewhere in the Bronx.

One of Philip's dreams was for me to take his ashes to Puerto Rico and spread them on the beach near his mother's native village. But I failed him. I feel as if I failed him in this and much else.

## Toward Forgiveness

Philip's life has, in the years since he's died, become a kind of strange and comforting beacon and example to me. Reflecting on his dreams, his fiercely held loves and hates, his humor and intelligence, his instinct (nay, *genius*) for practical action, his continuing day-to-day commitment to stay sober, I find more help and sustenance even now than I believe I ever managed to give him while he lived. Reflecting on his passionate contradictory life somehow gives me more reason to live and stay sober than I believe I was ever able to inspire in him. He has inspired me to look around at other gay men and lesbians who are living lives in recovery that are every bit as colorful and idiosyncratic and wildly explorative as he was in his own life. He has inspired me to question what exactly the rewards of sobriety are, leading me to see that they are not as simple or clear to discern as I once thought. In short, Philip continues to teach me so much about the ingenuity we bring to sober life—an ingenuity that seems especially, particularly, and excitingly evident in the lives of lesbians and gay men.

What atonement can I make for backing out of Philip's life just when he needed me most? I'm not sure. All I know how to do is to pass on something of the richness and mystery of his story and the richness and mystery of the stories of other gay men and lesbians that his example has prodded me to explore.

"Making amends," which various of the Twelve Steps in Twelve Step programs prepare and encourage us to do on a moment-by-moment basis, is, Philip's example teaches me, quite essentially *ongoing*. Nothing we do to bolster and maintain our sobriety is finite; no decision we make can ever be made once and for all. Sobriety, like consciousness (which has always seemed to be a synonym for sobriety), like life itself, is a stream of momentary feelings, thoughts, and decisions. We maintain it moment by moment, attempting to embrace each new circumstance with as open a heart and mind as we can muster up. Sobriety depends for its sustenance on an essential flexibility—an essential ability to *respond* in the open and childlike way Philip was sometimes able to respond when he allowed other people's pain to touch him, as well as to forgive ourselves when it seems all we can call up are the kinds of vengeful fantasies Philip occasionally wreaked on his noisy, drunken neighbors, but which more often simply tore his own heart apart. Sobriety teaches us we can survive anything— including our own inevitable fears, rages, and fallibilities.

As I near another anniversary of the moment I picked up and put down my last drink of alcohol and as I reflect on my own fallibilities (now painfully vivid to me as I reflect on Philip and my faltering connection to him), I'm more than ever struck by the amazing capacity for healing that, as recovering gay men and lesbians have taught me, we have access to in sobriety. I feel profound remorse about not coming through for Philip at the crucial hour, and yet I don't hate myself. I even believe I might be able to count on Philip's own forgiveness—and perhaps even on yours. That this forgiveness is available is proven to me whenever I hear a gay or lesbian recovering addict talk about his or her daily triumphs and travails. An open-eyed forgiveness is part of the lifeblood we give to each other, enriching our connections to each other, deepening the commitment to stay sober.

## Letting Life Happen

Connection, yes, but also diversity. That's central to what we stand to gain from and offer to each other. Loose and varied tribe though we are, gay men and lesbians have consistently been at the vanguard of creative recovery. We are an ingenious bunch, often mixing New Age approaches with any number of therapies in addition, sometimes (but not always), to the traditional Twelve Step route. We've forged many paths through the jungle.

Lesbians and gay men, as a group, have taught me that "sobriety" and "recovery" are enormously open-ended and encompassing terms. The sense of "forgiveness" that Philip unwittingly allowed me to stumble into is only part of this wider, more ambiguous, and ultimately more reassuring sense of recovery. "There is a point to being sober," Dorothy, with twenty years of sobriety, tells me, "and it's not just that you learn to keep from picking up a drink or a drug. It's that you've now got the chance to have life happen to you. And while that's not always fun, it's always illuminating. And, for me, so far, ultimately—and sometimes unbelievably—rewarding."

The women and men in this book all seem to me to be in the messy, revelatory process of recovering their capacity not only to live without resorting to alcohol or drugs but also to find ways to grow and feel joy that may take them pretty far afield—even out of, maybe even never having been in, Twelve Step programs. Even if AA or NA or any other "A" continues to have value, it may mean different things as you go on. In fact, it's common for long-term Twelve-Steppers to find that their approach to "program" evolves over time, sometimes causing them to make very idiosyncratic accommodations to the Steps and Traditions. "I stopped beating myself up for not doing a 'perfect' Fourth Step, the one about doing a fearless moral inventory," Esther, an AA-goer with twelve years of sobriety says. "I've accepted that right now I go to meetings for companionship and camaraderie and the dose of self-honesty I always get after a meeting. I've grown to respect how I'm evolving—I trust my own responses to AA, and to life, a lot more. I'm making it work for me, no matter what it looks like to anybody else. This is probably the most freeing sense I've gotten over the years: that I truly am the architect of my own life, that the only answers that make sense are the ones I come to on my own. This is not some abstract exercise, either. I've just been through a major wrangle with the IRS. I've lost two jobs in the past ten years right when I was in the most debt. These were all situations that once would have sent me careening into a bar or to my local drug dealer. But somehow I've learned to keep my eyes open, to listen to as much information from the world and from my own heart as I can without judging it—simply to see, as clearly as I can, what's really happening, what I'm really feeling, what both my outer and inner realities are trying to tell me. I've learned that pain does after all prod growth. And somehow I feel more alive for having gone through all this disappointment. Amazingly, the capacity to tolerate darkness has also increased my capacity to tolerate and rejoice in light. Whatever furrows have been dug in me by life in recovery always finally turn out to be fertile. Something gets planted even after the most terrible storms. And something new always grows."

Other people have taken different routes from the Twelve Step programs, such as undergoing psychotherapy, engaging in a variety of private inner spiritual journeys, cultivating support from family and friends, changing nutritional habits, dealing with depression with medication, or paying attention to other "addictive" areas—such as sexual compulsion, workaholism, and overeating—that can crop up with unnerving ferocity long into sobriety. And, as I've suggested, gay men and lesbians have been at the forefront of exploring what often turn out to be mix-and-match approaches to sustaining sobriety, questioning received dogma, and creating new ways to connect and combat the killing isolation that fuels the soul sickness of addiction.

## Duplicity: The Inside Track

Walk into any largely heterosexual "Beginners" AA meeting, and you'll still hear a common moan of complaint about the shame of admitting we're "addicted." For many heterosexuals, saying "I am an alcoholic" or "I am an addict" is the first time they've had to confront the prospect and feeling of being stigmatized—the first time they've had to separate themselves from the wider pack of humanity. Most lesbians and gay men are already old hands at this sense of feeling "apart"; we understand from our own frequent past experience of having to hide our sexuality or sexual feelings what it means to have a divided self—a public self and a hidden, often shameful inner self. This long-entrenched feeling of duplicity doesn't perhaps give us a leg up on everyone else, but by the time we admit our addictions and start to seek help to deal with them, our nearly lifelong senses of "divided self" have, often, already given us the ability to empathize with the pain others who aren't gay often feel and express as they ram, for what may feel like the first conscious moments in their lives, into their own exasperating inner (secret, shameful) and outer (more public and circumscribed) divisions of self. Many gay men and lesbians pass on the welcome news that all this inner/outer stuff is human and normal—more than that, that sobriety can help us to *embrace* our unnerving divisions.

When we make it to recovery, tired from so many years of feeling we had to hide who we were, exhausted from all the half-truths or out-and-out lies we felt we had to tell about our romantic and professional dreams and aspirations, we typically want more from sobriety than just the ability to say no to addictive substances and behaviors. "Recovery" affords us new opportunities for growth that go far beyond throwing out Valium pills or vodka bottles; recovering, we beckon to ourselves to look at, be curious about, perhaps even (ultimately) acknowledge and accept what we may once guiltily have labeled and dismissed as the "dark" sides of our personalities. This desire for a more complete self-acceptance is often what made us want to "recover" in the first place: we yearn to recover the capacity to tolerate, to be, *all of who we are*. Pursuing this new, lively, conscious psychic unity seems to be the deeper and wider aim of sobriety—the achievement of which depends on a lot more than simple abstinence from drugs or alcohol.

This larger aim will take us into some surprising realms and enable us to make connections to the deeper underlying pain and hunger that always fuel compulsive and addictive behavior. "There's no doubt that whatever alcoholic epiphany I had—and it really was what AA calls a spiritual awakening—that enabled me to stop drinking changed my life," one forty-five-year-old gay man named Mark says. "It opened doors I never knew were there. But now, five years down the road, I still feel like I'm in uncharted territory. I'm not sure that if I'd known how bewildering life would be, back when I first stopped drinking, I would have looked forward so happily to a 'life in sobriety.' Maybe that initial ignorance really was bliss—it helped that I didn't know what was coming up, that all I had to do was get through day after day without drinking. But, after about three years of steady attendance at AA meetings, I really felt I'd outgrown a lot of the triage elements of it: I began to resent the kind of kindergarten slogans that had once been so helpful to me: 'Easy does it,' 'Keep it simple,' 'One day at a time,' and the rest. As my ability to function in the world improved, I began to spend more time with people who had no idea what alcoholism was. I really felt 'cured.' However, as more years have gone by, I've been so humbled by the hunger that is at the root of my alcoholism—the hunger for 'more' which did not go away when I put down the bottle. I do sometimes still think I'm a different species from the 'normal' people who aren't besieged by this hunger. And sometimes I've felt unbelievably alone."

How Mark has learned to deal with this aloneness constitutes one of many paths that *Vastly More Than That* will attempt to illuminate: "Going back to AA meetings sometimes helps—especially meetings geared to gay people—just because it reminds me that I'm not alone after all. But this 'hunger for more' has also propelled me into new avenues. I've returned to Judaism, for example, which amazes my Orthodox parents—and my gay friends who dismiss all religion as homophobic. I grew up hating the 'chosen people' idea that I felt my parents fed me all through childhood. All the stuff you had to do—separating meat and dairy dishes, the whole kosher shtick—just seemed like nonsense to me, not to mention the horror that Orthodox and Conservative Jews typically have of homosexuality. But now I've joined a Jewish spiritual discussion group that includes both gay and straight men and women, and I'm getting so much out of the idea of the sanctification of daily life, which is at the root of Jewish religious observance. That there is something holy about each moment of life is somehow a tremendously nourishing idea to me. It's something I really want to explore. Exploring it is, I realize, one of my main methods right now of keeping sober. I don't want to blot out consciousness, not when it seems to promise so much. That would be stupid. Drinking again wouldn't give me anything I need. It would deprive me of what I need. I know that now on what seems like an inarguably practical level."

I hope in these pages finally to strike a resoundingly hopeful chord: the experience of ongoing sobriety has tremendous lessons to teach us about tolerating and overcoming the inevitable fear, pain, and anger anyone faces in life simply by continuing to exist on the planet—not to mention the intensified fears and rages that, with our addictive behaviors, we often desperately seek to cover up or deny. However, there are rarely simple or easy ways to combat these demons of fear and rage; in fact, depending on drugs or alcohol may for many years be the sole way our psyches know of fighting them. We don't escape in the ways that we do for no reason. As destructive and self-destructive as addictions may appear to others, unconsciously we resort to them to cure our pain, not intensify it. This view of addictive behavior as an attempt at self-cure needs to be honored.

For example, Lena, a lesbian with fourteen years of sobriety, realizes that her drinking and drug-taking were once profoundly necessary defenses to her. "They were a way of medicating myself against some horrifically violent feelings in me," she says. "And while I managed to stay sober for a good ten years before I had a breakdown four years ago, that experience was like a tidal wave that had been gaining power all through those ten years. It felt like a terrible black volcano erupted—it just took ten years actually to explode." Lena ended up in a psychiatric hospital when one morning she simply stopped working at her civil service job, sat at her desk with her head in her hands, and proceeded to cry, without ceasing, for the rest of the day. "When any of my co-workers tried to touch me, move me, talk to me, I reacted like a rabid animal," Lena says. "I lashed out at them—physically shoved them away. Beneath this terrible sadness was what felt like a bottomless pit of rage." Finally she was taken away in a straitjacket by medics whom her boss summoned from a local psychiatric hospital. "The blackness I was in was indescribable,"

Lena says today. "I was literally unreachable for weeks. I wouldn't respond to anyone, wouldn't talk to anyone. All I would do was cry. I felt like some terrible trapped animal; there was nothing that could possibly calm it or set it free. They gave me Haldol, an anti-psychotic drug, which did eventually calm me down, but I still couldn't speak to anyone. But being drugged again was somewhat appeasing. I vaguely remember thinking that at least *something* was softening the edge of the agony I was in."

A visit from her sister elicited the first sign of response in Lena. "Seeing this one member of my family I loved marked my first step back to consciousness," Lena says. "There was a look in her eyes of such unconditional caring—I don't know. I guess another, gentler spring in me erupted. I began to talk again. I began to let out this incoherent mass of feelings that had been so backed up in me. I'd hidden my sexuality from everyone in my family, but I somehow found the courage to come out to my sister. And it was amazing. She simply sat there and listened, and then tentatively reached out to touch my hand when I was done with my tirade. She'd been warned by the nurse not to touch me because I'd become violent before whenever anyone actually physically touched me. But she must have known how much I craved contact—the flip side of my rage and fear was an immense hunger for love. Slowly, I began the climb back up to being able to function. I'm now seeing a psychoanalyst who, actually, reminds me of my sister, and I'm on Zoloft, the antidepression drug. The worst of the blackness has gone. But I've emerged with a tremendous respect for the forces and drives inside me, and how I can't do what I used to do anymore—push them down, ignore them, pretend that I'm self-sufficient and I don't need anyone. I do need, and I'm learning I can express that need. How does this relate to my sobriety? It relates absolutely. Sobriety is just another word for being conscious. Not drinking or drugging wasn't enough. I had to release the other vises I'd tightened in myself: I had to find a way to let out the lava in me so that it wouldn't kill me. I guess the greatest lesson from all this is that I don't have to seek out those channels alone. Medication can help me. Psychoanalysis can help me. My sister can help me. I'm even slowly growing to believe I might be able to make some friends again—even maybe find and live with a lover. It's as if I had to learn on a much deeper level what I realized when I first put down drugs and alcohol: 'cure' comes from feeling connected, from acknowledging the fierce needs and loneliness in me, not from trying to deny them."

## Only Connect

*Connection*: once again, there are so many seeds of help and healing in that word. Indeed, the connections lesbians and gay men have made to each other in sobriety have given me, perhaps, the strongest reason to compile our stories and to fulfill what I see as Philip's legacy. There has been far too much separateness in the way gay men and women traditionally have approached and thought about each other. Too often we react to each other as if we were entirely different species—for example, buying lesbian "urge-to-merge" and gay male "screw-anything-that-moves" stereotypes without questioning them, without realizing that so much in our experience actually *joins* us far more than separates us. Philip was not someone I would have gone out of my way to know on my own. It was his quest, and ultimately my quest, to sustain our own and each other's sobriety, to explore what "sobriety" *meant* to each of us, that forged the links between us and taught both of us that there were more points of contact between us than we had ever suspected. (Philip realized this before I did; it was why he sought me out—because he recognized something in me that mirrored his own struggles, hopes, and illuminations.)

This is just as richly true about the connections between gay men and women, connections that wait to be found and explored and celebrated.

However, I cannot hope in this book to have done more than touch on some of the surprising ways our emotional lives and experiences as lesbians and gay men are similar: filling out the map is something each of you reading this book must do on your own, adding your own experience and the experiences of the people you know in your recovering life to the men's and women's lives you'll touch in this book. All I can guarantee is that there are more connections between us than we start out realizing there are, more ways to *grow* than we knew when we first put down that last drug or drink and decided to face life without blotting out our minds and hearts.

As you discover the paths various gay men and lesbians have taken in this pursuit of conscious life, please add your own story to the mix and share the inevitably rich result with someone—like me, like Philip—who started out thinking "connection" was all but impossible. Teach each other that our hearts will always recognize true pain and love and healing, no matter what "gay" or "lesbian" trappings they wear. We have so much to give each other. Think of this book as an invitation to open up the floodgates in your own hungry soul, so that you can let your gift out and let someone else's gift in. "Analyze" in the widest, most affirming—even sometimes joyous—sense that the Twelve Steps and our own hungry, curious hearts beckon us to do. There's always more in front of your nose, or just under the surface, than you think.

At one particularly low point when I was broke and hated my work and hated everybody I knew and saw no recourse or hope or chance of change whatsoever (and this was after ten years of sobriety), I told my analyst I felt like a baby dumped into a sandbox and left there without so much as a bottle. (I was thinking milk, but my unconscious mind probably meant vodka.) Uncharacteristically (he rarely gave me advice), he made a suggestion.

"Dig around," he said. "There's more in your sandbox than you think."

It turned out he was right.

# 2 The Secret Strangeness of the Twelve Steps

"You know what gets me?" Stan, twenty-four and (as he puts it) "stranded" in a small farm town in western Pennsylvania, asks rhetorically. "Just about every book addressed to gay people seems to assume we live in New York or San Francisco or Los Angeles. Like I could walk down my street in chaps and a leather harness hand in hand with RuPaul and nobody would notice or care. Well, I don't live anywhere like that. I'm in rural Pennsylvania. And, believe me, there's no S&M activist group down the block of my hometown. There's not even a gay bar within a radius of two hundred miles. Until I got a computer and started to talk to people on the Internet, I was beginning to think I was the only gay person in the state, apart from a few furtive, supposedly straight guys I ran into at our community college."

Certainly Stan's recourse for help and information regarding recovery—at least until he got on-line—was clearly limited to the weekly AA meeting in the basement of his Lutheran church. "About nine people go, seven men; five of them are farmers; one of them runs the drug store—he's my uncle, the guy who got me in here—and another guy who doesn't have a job right now, the youngest one other than me, who's about forty-three. Then there are two sisters in their fifties. They're all married. And they're all, shall we say, less than liberal. Several of them keep trying to hook me up with their daughters. I just smile and keep saying I'll 'turn it over.' Plus the fact that my uncle's in the group tends to shut me up—I mean, even if I had the guts to tell them what I was really torn up about, my sexuality, I just couldn't bring myself to do it with my uncle listening in."

Despite the constraints of being gay and going to AA in a small town, the meeting has still helped Stan. "So what if I have to translate everything I hear into something that relates to me as a gay man? Maybe there's something good about feeling some sort of common thread to all these straight guys—I mean, when they talk about craving a drink, well, I don't have to translate that. I know what they're saying. And there's a good deal of wisdom in the group. My sponsor is one of the oldest guys; he's actually the man who started AA here. He's real by-the-book. I suspect he knows more about me than he lets on. I mean, when I did a Fourth Step with him, that moral inventory thing, I know he knew I was leaving some things out—the sex parts. But he didn't ride me for it. 'Some stuff is harder to say than other stuff,' he tells me. 'That's why you get to do this Step again and again. More will come out. Give it time. Just remember, you're only as sick as your secrets.'

"At first when he said that to me, I turned white. I thought it meant he could see right through me. I thought he meant that I was sick because I was gay. But it's almost like he read my mind. At least, he seemed to know the right thing to say to reassure me: 'It's not the secret that's sick. It's *keeping* it secret that's the problem; that's what makes you *feel* sick. Like, for instance, now. You ain't turnin' white because you're choking on your coffee, Stan, are you?' He smiled and we made a joke of it and then he left it at that and I felt somehow, somehow, all this would turn out okay. 'Give time time,' he said. I've never been sure what that meant. But it soothed me. I don't know; I guess you get more from a person's tone of voice sometimes than from whatever words he uses.

My sponsor calms me down every time I hear his voice. It's quiet and deep, and I can't imagine him ever losing his temper. Maybe that's why I ended up trusting him a little more than I do anybody else in my AA group, even before I actually came out to him."

But Stan was not otherwise calm. "I'd gone for a couple of years to a community college not too far away, but that didn't bring me any closer to open gay life, even if it was where I had my first sexual experiences with men." Stan discovered a peculiarly busy men's room in the basement of the school's library. "At first I thought there was some epidemic of diarrhea going around," he says. "These guys all kept going down there, staying there a long time, and then going downstairs to the toilet again and again. Not too many students, although there were about a half dozen college kids who sometimes seemed to spend most of their afternoons down there. But like, I don't know, truck drivers from the interstate and married businessmen and who knows who—all these men made this sort of pilgrimage to the library basement men's room. I guess everyone thought I was straight, because every time I walked in, zippers closed, taps ran, stall doors closed—they obviously wanted to hide whatever they were doing from me. But then finally this one guy standing at a urinal—one of the businessmen, about thirty-five I guess, had a wedding ring—didn't zip up when I walked in and gave me a clear view of what his right hand was stroking. I was riveted. He motioned for me to come over. And, well—"

Furtive meetings with this man several times more in this bathroom, then in an unused office Stan knew how to get into on the third floor, and then in the woods outside town constituted the sum and total of Stan's experience of sex and relationships. "We'd meet a lot in the woods in the summer," Stan says, "and he'd always bring a flask of something like 80 proof vodka. It was the only thing that calmed him down, I guess, that made him re-laxed enough to go through with what he obviously wanted to do. I don't think we ever said more than three words to each other. We just 'did it.' I was happy to share the booze, even though I'd never tasted a drop of alcohol before that moment. I guess I was as freaked as he was, really—hell, I was only eighteen—and I knew, boy, if anybody needed to relax, it was me. And I loved the taste of alcohol from the first gulp out of that flask. It was like some secret potion nobody had ever told me about before. It let you do all the nasty sex things you couldn't bring yourself to do any other way. I was carrying pint bottles of vodka around every-where I went. It was my medication, I told myself—something to calm down before class, before doing my laundry, before calling my mother, but of course mostly help me to lose my inhibitions so that I could have sex with that married man again."

By the time Stan was twenty, he'd wrecked two cars, which put him in the hospital for a total of ten months: "Broke my collar-bone, left leg, bad concussion, sprained right ankle—you name it, I broke or almost broke it. After the second hospital stay, my uncle literally took me by the ear to the town AA meeting and made me sit next to him. He didn't tell me where he was taking me; he just said, 'Come with me.' I was amazed seeing the other men there. I knew all of them, of course, but I had no idea why any of them would be sitting together in this room." The nature of the meeting soon became clear, and Stan surprised his uncle at the end of it by thanking him. "I actually loved being there. I loved hearing the stories. I don't think I identified with any of them, really, but I'd never heard a group of men say such emo-tional and honest stuff! I just wanted to be around them. If the password was that I had to say I was an alcoholic, that was fine. Which I guess brings up the stronger motive for wanting to stay—and stop drinking. I'd always associated drinking with my 'nasty homosexual acts.' I truly thought that if I never drank again, I'd not only never have a homosexual encounter again, but I'd never feel the urge again." Stan's eyes roll up. "Oh, when I think of how little I knew. . . ." He pauses, then looks back at me. "Or how little I know now, I guess."

Stan's uncle was a little shocked—and suspicious—that Stan embraced AA so early. Few alkies in his experience ever "saw the light" *that* quickly. But Stan's resolve stuck. His uncle simply didn't know that what mostly made it stick was Stan's desperate hope that sobriety would turn him straight. The drinking wasn't the problem, Stan felt, as much as how it activated his "evil" desires and made him do the worst, most abominable thing—have sex with men. "Maybe you don't realize how strong church is out here," Stan says, expecting what he usually gets when he tells someone less closeted his story (variations on "Oh come on; you can't really mean you ever thought *that*. I mean, we're thirty years past Stonewall!"). "My pastor and my parents made hell seem like a very real place to me— and one you could very well end up in if you were a homosexual."

"Then I got my computer," Stan says. "Actually, when I'd been in the hospital, there was a patient recreation area with a bunch of fairly up-to-date computers we could use if we wanted to when we had the time. This one plump young nurse had a crush on me, I think; she taught me the basics. I learned how to get on-line, and I've never gotten off. In some ways, I think, for a while it did what vodka used to do for me, gave me a sort of safe escape where I could say things I never could have said at home, and it allowed me to talk to real, actual, non-self-hating gay people for the first time in my life. In other words, I found out how to tap into all the gay chat lines. And, *whoa*—is rural Pennsylvania different than I thought it was!"

There turned out to be many lesbians and gay men in the towns dotting his half of the state and, Stan says, "We sort of had this running fraternity-sorority, with club meetings three nights a week. It was so neat not only because it was the first time I'd ever actually talked to another gay man instead of just have sex with him. It was also the first time I'd ever met any lesbians. There were lesbians in Pennsylvania small towns! It blew me away. But we talked like friends talked; it wasn't all about sex, or even mostly about sex. It was about hiding, mostly—how much we had to keep away from everyone else in our lives. One school-teacher was afraid he'd be fired; one divorced mother made herself go out with men so that no one would suspect what was really going on between her and her live-in roommate—I don't know. There was a whole world out there of gay men and lesbians talking to each other. It was wonderful, but it was also almost disastrous, in a way."

The almost-disaster was simply this: "Everyone seemed to *drink* so much," Stan says. "Almost every exchange had stuff about 'how drunk I got last night' and 'thank God for pot; otherwise I couldn't cope' and 'you mean you can get through a day without Atavan?' I don't know; it was sort of like what I was afraid of before when I gave up vodka. I mean I finally realized— duh!—that I'd be gay whether or not I drank, but drinking and getting high were as big an obsession for so many gay men and women as sex was. And I realized I wasn't so different. Before I wanted to stop drinking to stop being gay. Now I was beginning to want to start drinking *to* be gay—to have sex again. Vodka and sex were completely linked in my mind. I began to think, God, there's no way I'll ever have sex again if I *don't* drink. It was like, you can't have one without the other."

When Stan zapped a few lines at his Internet buddies to this effect, he said, "It was like I'd found the magic words. Everybody agreed. And everybody thought there was simply no other way to do it. Couldn't have sex without getting high. At least and have it be good." Stan was secretly thrilled: "It turned out I wasn't the only one! Lots of gay people got high to have sex. It got me thinking very differently about drinking.

"I hadn't told anyone I went to AA—again, I didn't really think of myself as alcoholic. The meeting was just someplace I could go and hear a group of men talk about something other than tractors or the early frost or federal taxes. Being 'alcoholic' was the price of admission." But now the Internet was beginning to replace AA in his interests and affections. "My uncle wouldn't let me stop going to meetings, and my sponsor made it clear that he thought it would be a very good idea if I stuck around 'one day at a time.' But my mind wandered. What I really had started to think about in meetings was, now that I'm less self-hating, won't I abuse vodka less? Maybe the problem was that 'internalized homophobia' that weirdo lesbian Kirin kept going on about on-line. Now that I liked myself more, I could take a drink or get high, couldn't I? The truth was, I was desperate to have sex with someone. I'd been getting sort of romantic with two of the guys on-line and they weren't that far away—just an hour by car. Why couldn't I—why shouldn't I—pick up a quart of Popov on the way?"

Stan began daydreaming about this possibility every time he went to an AA meeting. He continued to "work the Steps" with his sponsor, John—which John required as a condition of taking Stan on as sponsee—and every week they'd meet and talk about whatever Step they were up to. Stan had gotten into the habit of jotting down into a notebook whatever events or feelings the upcoming Step brought up in him right before meeting with John, which John encouraged him to do. He always kept these notes "gay-free" since he'd always open and read from the notebook in full view of John's very straight eyes. "I often felt like I was preparing some kind of Sunday school homework assignment where I had to be sure not to use any really shocking words.

Certainly, it never occurred to me that I could ever tell my sponsor what I used to do with a thirty-five-year-old married man in the woods outside my college."

But after two or three weeks of daydreaming about the renewed possibilities of Popov vodka-as-aphrodisiac, he couldn't help writing POPOV on the top of the page. "I didn't even realize I'd done it. It just sort of came out of me, like a doodle. Anyway, we did the Steps in an endless cycle and we were once again on Step Three—for probably the tenth time. I always looked at the Steps exactly like I used to look ahead to whatever class was coming up in junior high: would it be easy, like art, or hard, like algebra? The Third Step was one of the easy ones. It's the Step that everyone in my AA group seemed to like too. 'Made a decision to turn our will and our lives over to the care of God *as we understood Him.*' I eased back in my chair, I remember, as I opened my notebook and laid it flat on the table: this was going to be a nice easy night—John and I would just sort of sit back and meditate on 'letting go.' I started to think of all sorts of comforting things like surrendering and letting my Higher Power take care of everything. The Third Step could feel like a nice warm bath; it almost felt like taking a drink, sometimes! It didn't make you *do* anything, like that awful Step that said you had to go out and make amends to everybody. *That* was like calculus—or root canal. But we were in lala land now, thank God. And I was about to open my mouth about how good it would feel just to 'let go let God' and stop worrying so much about everything when John cut me off."

John was looking and then pointed his right index finger at the elaborately lettered heading on the page open in front of both of them. He asked: "What's this?" Stan groaned inwardly as he finally registered that, without realizing it, he'd inked out a careful POPOV. *"I didn't know I'd done it!* That's what really freaked me out. At first I panicked, like John could somehow read my mind—

like he could see I was fantasizing about drinking vodka and having sex with a man. Then I thought, *Don't be stupid.* I could explain it without blurting all that out. It wouldn't be that hard. I mean, I was supposed to be alcoholic. Of course I'd think sometimes about vodka. I could just say I was remembering my last drunk or something. So I started to tell him that Popov was the brand of vodka I'd last gotten blitzed on, and he stopped me. 'No, I know what Popov is,' John said. 'I wasn't asking about that. I was asking about *this.*'"

Stan's eyes widened in horror as he watched his sponsor pull out the separated centerfold from a copy of the gay male porno magazine *Mandate* that one of his Internet friends had mailed him, which he thought he'd carefully locked back into his safe deposit box in his room but instead had left folded right under the notebook page, one perfectly tan-lined right white butt cheek of which had now slipped out from the notebook and into his conservative heterosexual middle-aged small-town sponsor's hand.

Stan remembers being more shocked—even panicked—about his having forgotten that he had left the centerfold in the notebook he was taking to his God-fearing Lutheran sponsor than he was about the prospect of explaining a gay porno centerfold to him: "Another outrageous thing I did without realizing it! Was I losing my mind? It was like some weird part of me wanted to sabotage the works—reveal all my shameful secrets to show what a horrible sick beast I really was. I literally couldn't speak. And when John quickly realized he had decidedly not pulled out a centerfold from *Playboy*, he grew quiet too. He slipped the glossy male ass back into the notebook. He took a sip of cocoa. Then he looked at me with steady eyes and asked me, quietly: 'So. What's up?'

"I said nothing. I couldn't think of anything to say, and my mouth wouldn't work. I couldn't believe what had happened. It was like some switch at the center of me got flipped off: I just went numb. I probably was literally in some state of shock. John spoke again, gently: 'Remember, it's not what the secret's about as much as the *secrecy*.' His words registered a little bit through the wad of cotton batting my brain had become. I was distantly aware of being surprised that John wasn't attacking me for my unspeakable sins and immorality, which I was convinced—probably rightly—I could have expected from just about everyone else in that Lutheran town. Something in me sort of felt like it had softened a little, but *only* a little. I was still stunned and I guess still terrified. We sat there in silence probably only for ten or so seconds, but it felt like a year."

Stan lets out a little rueful laugh. "Man, if this were a movie of the week or something, I would have burst into tears and told John everything I'd been holding back, and John would have comforted me and told me it was okay and there was no reason to feel so bad, and I'd be amazed that he was so understanding, and maybe I *could* live happily as a gay man after all." Stan's face tenses a bit: "But what really happened was, I made a croaking sound. Then I rasped at him that I thought I'd better go.

"'Let's start on the Fourth Step next week,' John said to me, as gently as ever, somehow managing to catch my eye for a second—no easy feat given how determined I was to avoid looking into his face. I didn't speak—that ability had dried up in my throat again; it felt now like for good—but I was convinced he could somehow hear every last sneering tone of the words that were ringing away in my head: 'Yeah, *right*. I'm really going to hand you a list of all the times I've gotten sucked off by a married businessman in my next Fourth Step.'"

Stan left John's kitchen convinced not only that he was leaving AA forever and would never again come back to talk about anything with John, much less a "fearless moral inventory" of his unspeakable sins, but that the next best thing he could possibly do would be to make a stop at the liquor store. "It's weird—maybe I really was having some psychotic break. The only picture in my mind was so stupid; it didn't seem to have anything to do with anything! It was that plump baker in the Dunkin' Donuts commercial, the one who's always chanting, 'It's time to make the doughnuts!' Well, there he was again; only now he was chanting, 'It's time to buy the Popov.'"

## The DF/VD Correspondence

Stan got into his car outside his sponsor's house; it was just about five o'clock. It occurred to him: in a simple two-hour car drive, he could get himself back to that men's room in the college library. He tried not to think of what had just happened: "It was like something in me shut down. Like I was just refusing to think of my sponsor or anything at all that would upset me." Instead he thought about what he ought to wear. There was that sexy black T-shirt he had at home. And the worn ripped blue jeans that hugged his butt really nicely. He decided to go home and change before he picked up the Popov.

"I got home and started looking for the clothes I wanted to wear, and suddenly I felt almost fluey, a little spaced—like I needed just to rest for a moment. So I flopped down on my bed, but I couldn't untense. I looked over to the computer on my desk. Maybe I could kill this feeling by getting on-line. Do something to distract me."

He found his favorite RFDLGM chat group (RFD Lesbians & Gay Men, code word HICK HOMOS) and many of the usuals were on-line. Stan says he found himself typing, on an impulse, as if out of nowhere: "I'm about to get trash drunk and suck dick in a college library men's room. Anyone wanna COME? If you get my meaning." Computer equivalents of hoots and hollers soon flooded the screen. Followed by a terse commandment from the chat's leading lesbian feminist, Kirin (aka VD), which read simply: "PRIVATE CHAT.NOW." Stan says he flashed on how once, months before, in response to some diatribe Kirin had just spat out, someone unkind on-line called her Vagina Dentata. Far from taking offense, Kirin thought it was hilarious, thanked him effusively, and immediately adopted it as a sobriquet. Stan says she especially loved its initials, VD. "She was one tough cookie," Stan says. "But something about her command grabbed out at me, challenged me. It was like, I felt so friggin' arrogant and confident at that moment, I could even take on ol' Vagina Dentata. 'Give me your best shot, VD. I can take it.' Something like that. Anyway, I said sure and we removed ourselves from the group. And she fired away."

Stan takes out a beaten-looking sheaf of papers and opens it. "I managed to print out that conversation and others after it," Stan says. "Here. Look at the first couple pages."

They ran something like this:

VD:      YOU DUMB FUCK!

S:      Excuse me?

VD:      You're going to blow your damn sobriety, asshole.

S:      Excuse me?

VD:      Stop saying, Excuse me. I won't excuse you. I had you pegged from the moment you got online. You know how many times you said stuff like Keep it simple and Turn it over? Don't tell me you're not in AA. But don't tell me you're going to do something as STUPID as blow it so you can blow some stranger at a urinal. Come on. You gotta be smarter than that.

34

s:    Are you in AA?

VD:    OF COURSE, DUMB FUCK!!!

s:    I wish you'd stop calling me that.

VD:    Then stop being one. Look, screw yourself blind—I try to all the time—but don't assume that the only way you can do it is blind drunk. I've had better, hotter, more wonderful sex sober than I ever did high. Not despite the lack of booze and drugs but because of it. In fact, I was just telling a sponsee that the best sex guide I've ever read is the Big Book.

s:    You sure you're not high now?

VD:    You think I'm kidding. Man, dance those Steps right and you'll end up a stud. Of course, some dance steps are harder than others.

s:    Yeah, like making amends to your grandmother for beating off in her fine linen sheets.

VD:    Oh no. That's easy. It's the "turn it over" one that's hard.

s:    I was just thinking the opposite: That the Third Step is almost like having a drink. Letting it all go. Pretty close to what I used to say before I drank a quart of Popov. Only then I said, "Fuck it."

VD:    Boy are you clueless.

s:    What makes you think you're so smart?

VD:    I know what I know. I know when I'm hearing crap. And what I'm hearing right now is crap.

s:    Excuse me?

VD:    Imagine what it would be like to be totally and uninhibitedly WILLING. Imagine turning yourself into nothing but an open door, all eyes and ears:

total receptivity. Fearless, in a total state of trust. You can do that?

S: Yeah, when I'm drunk.

VD: When you were drunk, you were in a complete state of UNWILLINGNESS. Unwilling to see, feel, think. Unwilling to live. Unwilling to exist. You know that's true. What you were after was not to feel anything at all—not open yourself to feeling everything.

S: Who wants to feel everything? Anyway, vodka freed me to have sex.

VD: No it didn't. It made you numb. Numb enough to stop hating yourself for a moment so that you wouldn't care so damned much what you did. Actually, it locked you up, kept you from feeling what you could have felt. You know how you know you're doing the Third Step? When you've had a terrific, earth-shattering orgasm. When you FEEL what you're doing with your whole body and soul. THEN you know you've let go.

S: Boy, would I love you to speak at my AA meeting.

VD: Don't underestimate those farm boys. That mean you're going back? Not going out to get trash drunk?

S: I think so. Suddenly I'm feeling real tired.

VD: You got a sponsor?

S: Not one I ever feel like talking to again.

VD: Sounds perfect. Means you desperately want to tell him the truth but are too scared to open your mouth. Welcome to Planet Earth. Call him now.

So began what Stan calls the "DF/VD Correspondence" ("DUMB FUCK," Stan explains, "in case you didn't get the DF"), which continues to this day and which has slowly transformed Stan's view of not only what sobriety might mean (to him), but what being a conscious human being might mean (to him).

"She just blew me away," Stan says. "It's like she turned everything I used to think about 'program' and Twelve Step words like 'character defects,' 'surrender,' and 'Higher Power' into something completely different. The weird thing was, as outrageous as she got—like calling the Big Book a terrific sex guide—I somehow knew, right then and there, what she meant. I'm not sure I always agreed, but I could hear her, understand her, and that—that feeling of connecting to someone, the idea that you could actually *communicate* with somebody else, someone who I thought was so different from me, this cartoon of a militant lesbian—I don't know; maybe that's what blew me away most. But I *was* getting what VD said to me.

"I told her about how I'd lettered POPOV without realizing it and left a porno centerfold right where my sponsor could see it—and how much it scared me that I could have done something like this without realizing it. Was I crazy? No, she said. My self was just trying to get out, and I wouldn't let it. So it would try to come out without letting the conscious part of me know. That sounded like a bunch of hooey to me first, but now it seems a lot more interesting and maybe even somewhat true.

"But the thing about VD is, I don't have to agree with her to feel energized by her. And one of the biggest things she's helped me to realize is that I had never made the Twelve Steps anything like my own, not the way she had. And that was what I had to do for them to have any meaning. It didn't matter if I ended up with the same conclusions as she did; it mattered that, as VD put it once, I 'wrestled' with the Steps, wrestled them to the mat, struggled with what I felt they meant, not what I thought they were 'supposed' to mean."

Stan didn't go to the liquor store and decided he didn't after all want to make a four-hour round-trip drive to the library men's room, either. He was amazed to find he'd untensed. Something about the outrageous VD had had an almost chiropractic effect on his back. "I felt strange—both like I wanted to sleep and like I'd woken up." When, the next morning, he decided to call his sponsor, he found he could do it without feeling shame. "I sometimes think VD gave me a spiritual awakening, which would make a good line to use the next time I tell my story at an AA meeting, huh? I mean, I wasn't walking around on a golden cloud or anything, but I was, I don't know, more *curious* in a way about the things she said and *curious* about what John, my sponsor, would say if I did tell him more of 'the truth.'"

John turned out to be equal to the task of hearing it. "He told me he was a little uncomfortable," Stan said, "but he said that was normal. 'Everybody's pretty unique, I guess,' is how he put it. And then he told me about this porno magazine he'd seen once on the newsstand in Harrisburg and how the big-breasted woman on the cover not only hadn't turned him on, but made him feel a little nauseated. Apparently, John liked women with small breasts. He was really actively turned off by all that excess chest. 'It bothered me a little,' John told me. 'Like I wasn't normal or something. Like a real man is supposed to like big boobs. But now I think, you like what you like. Doesn't matter whether everybody else does or doesn't.'" Stan smiles. "First of all, you gotta realize that John and I had never talked about sex before, and suddenly here I was finding out about his secret sexual likes and dislikes! It was unbelievable that this door had opened. I remembered what VD had said about the Third Step, about willingness. Somehow that door had opened a little wider between John and me."

VD's belief that the supposedly "scary" Steps—making that fearless moral inventory, telling it to your Higher Power and someone else back here on earth, making amends to the people you'd hurt—were really the easiest of all has taken Stan a little longer to understand. "But I sort of get it now," he says. "I mean, it's like what I just told you happened between John and me. When you're truly willing, you're not afraid. And when you're not afraid, anything is possible. So the thing that nearly gave me a stroke the night before—the idea of actually saying the words 'I'm gay' to John—was absolutely fine to tell him the next day, when I'd lost my fear: when I became *fearless*. As usual, VD reminded me of the definition of that word. When you're not afraid, she said, it doesn't mean you're brave. It means you're fearless—without fear. Brave means you're still really scared; you're standing up to your fear, but your fear's still there. Fearless means there's no fear at all. There's no need to be 'brave' because there's nothing to be afraid of." Stan blinks, exhales a whisper: *"What a concept. . . ."*

And the Third Step being hard? Does that seem true to him?

"Sort of. I mean, of course. Being in a total state of willingness, receptivity? That's like reaching nirvana or something. But, you know, after I had that first open talk with John, I realized not only that we *could* start talking about more difficult stuff with each other—not just about sex—but that I wanted to. So in a way it's not hard. I mean, it's become something I actually want to do. Something you want to do is a pleasure, not an obligation. Which pretty much gets to the heart of what VD keeps telling me: sobriety isn't a punishment; it's a reward. It makes you live *more* fully, not less.

"Sometimes it seems incomprehensible to me that a straight man and a lesbian are teaching me all this! How to be a gay man—a sober gay man—not to mention how the Big Book can improve your orgasms. But I guess that's part of the deal too. How much help there is out there from the strangest people. But also how important it is to figure out what you think about sobriety, what you think it means. Sounds obvious, but boy, it's amazing to start realizing how little I've done that, reflected on what things mean to me. Like VD said once, I see the whole world like some awful junior-high algebra class where I haven't done the homework, don't understand any of the exercises on the blackboard, and it's only a matter of time before the teacher finds me out and flunks me. But there's no teacher grading me; there's no blackboard; there's no algebra homework I have to do. *I'm* the teacher—and *I'm* the algebra, sort of—as well as the student."

Stan snorts at himself and apologizes: "Sorry, but this is how you start talking when you spend any time with VD. You start calling yourself algebra." He seems to reassemble himself: "What I mean is, *I'm* making so much of my own distress up. Most of what I'm afraid of—VD says *all* of what I'm afraid of—is phantoms in my head. What I'm not doing is letting go. VD's right. It's a lot harder to 'turn it over' than I used to think it was. As far as the part about how the Third Step can improve orgasms—well, I guess, as they say in my AA meeting, I'll just have to 'give time time.' But I gotta say, when I told John about the possible Big Book–Big O connection, he didn't look shocked or anything. Far from it. In fact, he said he could see how that just might be true."

## As the Prism Turns

So many gay men and lesbians who adhere in some manner to the Twelve Steps have had the same startling impact on me as

"VD" had on Stan. We so often make unusual connections, come up with singular interpretations, turn the prism on old saws (like the program slogan "Give time time" that we just heard Stan use in a rather interesting context!). At first, in search of an explanation, I happily entertained the self-flattering idea that gay people are just plain smarter than anybody else. Closer reflection told me that *that's* far from true (*I've* been awfully stupid more times than I can bear to remember, ran one quick rebuttal).

But we may tend to be ingenious in one particular, widely shared way, a way not as automatically shared by our heterosexual brothers and sisters. It does seem that we do tend, organically—seemingly spontaneously—to see things from interesting angles, an ability that often peculiarly enriches our experience in Twelve Step programs. Our ancient expertise at duplicity seems to give us this automatic understanding: *What you see on the surface probably isn't all that's going on.* And the experience of sustaining an outside self and an inner self, which very often begins in earliest childhood (Daddy's reaction to his three-year-old son asking for a Barbie doll has lifelong resonance), often eventually enables us to reflect on other people's divisions as well, helping us to understand that everyone (gay or not) has outer and inner levels, contradictions, and internal conflicts. It may also be why Messrs. Wilde, Coward, and Crisp—and so many of the rest of us—are so damned witty, or at least a richly appreciative audience for wit. Who appreciates the absurdity of pretense better than the Great Pretenders we have always had to be?

Not, God knows, that this understanding is always an unmitigated laugh riot. There can be—in fact, there always are—some pretty disturbing things below the surface, both in us and in others, that we'd often just as soon not see. And the "ancient duplicity" at which we're often so expert has a fundamentally tragic cause—it's the product, the scar, of a deep wound. You don't find it necessary to construct an "acceptable" outside self unless you learned that who you were *inside* was pretty contemptible. You don't do it because you're bored. You do it because you're terrified that anyone might ever learn who you really are. I don't have to tell you that's a pretty terrible way to feel.

But—as is the case with most wounds and most of what a shrink might label "neurotic"—the hurt can have its up side: an increased sensitivity to hidden currents in other people (gay or straight) and often an increased compassion for the conflict that anyone hiding a secret self always suffers. There may be so many gay people in "the helping professions" because we know how desperately and how deeply people need help. We know it because of our own urgent craving for it.

At the very least, this understanding of duplicity (good or bad in its causes and effects) does generally make us pretty good "translators," an ability that has very likely been honed to a sharp edge by the time you enter a Twelve Step meeting (if you do) and, for many of us who've kept going to meetings, has enriched our engagement with Twelve Step principles—even if we start out feeling, as VD once put it to Stan, that "the Big Book *is* a little like a 1940s Barbara Stanwyck and Fred MacMurray movie." It may take a bit of suspension of disbelief to turn Fred into Frederica or Barbara into Bob, but, hey—it's not like we haven't done it before.

"I'm so used to translating everything I see," Virginia says. "Or trying to. I mean, even though I wouldn't have labeled myself 'lesbian' when I was in my teens or even in my twenties, I knew something was really different in my response to the whole world—not just to men or women—from just about anyone around me. It was like, when I dutifully read through *Seventeen* magazine or *Cosmopolitan* like all the other girls and women I knew, I kept feeling: 'But that's not *true*—that's not what I want.' All those pep talks and warnings about what to say or what not to say to a man, how or how not to wear your hair, what a woman was and what she wasn't. I remember in college—this was back in the mid-seventies—how a bunch of girls who lived on my floor in the dorm would drift into my room, freshman year, not because of me, but because my roommate Sharon was so popular. It's like they wanted to study her, to try to find out everything she did so that they could be like her. 'Gee, where'd you get that beautiful blouse?' sort of thing. Or trying to find out without Sharon catching them what kind of nail polish she used, lipstick, perfume, all that—squinting quickly at her open vanity case when they walked nonchalantly into the room."

Virginia, forty-three, says she went to one of the "elitist" Seven Sister schools: "But although it was supposedly the middle of the swinging sexual revolution, and we were all supposed to be so smart and sophisticated and liberal, there weren't a lot of 'out' lesbians the way there are at Smith or Bryn Mawr now. The ones who were 'out' scared me. They really were so belligerent about it. I didn't feel like I was part of their tribe any more than I felt like Sharon or her adoring entourage. Even the smartest girls I knew sort of melted in front of Sharon, who was a pretty close ringer for Farrah Fawcett. But none of it fit me. Not that I knew what *did* fit. I just knew the world I was supposed to want to live in felt like Mars."

Virginia had one passion that, she said, saved her, one thing she could do that did make her feel at home, at least in herself. "I play the piano. I mean, I play it well enough that my teacher at Juilliard Prep—which I attended all through junior high and high school—said I should consider a career as a soloist. She had no illusions about how hard that was. She very rarely mentioned it as a serious possibility to any of her students. In fact, she said she'd only done it once before. That student is a pretty well-known concertizer today."

Virginia was deeply and soul-stirringly gratified by the assessment, but the idea terrified her. "I simply wasn't a performer. I hated audiences. I always played so much less than my best whenever I had to give a public recital. My teacher suggested taking Inderol to calm my nerves. It's even called the Juilliard pill: 'everybody takes it' is what I always heard there. In high school I began to take it too, and it helped, but I still didn't have whatever 'fire' you've got to have to start going out there and winning competitions. My teacher realized this and got off my back. But what I didn't get off was Inderol and the various other medications that slowly took its place."

By the time she was in college, Virginia had switched to Valium and took fairly heavy doses of it. She loved the fact that all it took to calm her down, to make her feel as if she could tolerate the world around her, was a pill. Or, as it soon transpired, *pills*. Many of them. She had established herself as a "sensitive type" with her psychiatrist-documented stage fright, and the college psychiatrist enabled her to keep up her Valium prescription "legitimately." "Of course, I could have gotten Valium and a whole lot more from various women in college. Slowly I connected with them—predictably arty types, wearing black. Heroin was starting to get chic then. I had a horror of sticking myself with a needle, although I was intrigued by what they said it felt like. But I didn't have the courage for it. I didn't have the courage for anything but what I already knew, which was pills. I certainly didn't feel any more at home with these underground *artistes* than I had with any other group of human beings I'd so far met, but at least they kept me mellow.

"I was taking barbiturates before long. I was missing classes before long. I was not waking up very often in the morning. I changed my major from chemistry, which I loved in high school but which was just suddenly too damned much of a nuisance in college, for obvious reasons. I switched to music history, which I already knew backwards and forwards. I'd pretty much stopped playing the piano. It was just too painful to sit down and realize how far I'd let myself lapse. I couldn't bear not being able to play what I used to be able to play with so little technical effort. I was so doped up most of the time that I couldn't get a simple Chopin waltz out without tripping all over it. When I think of it, playing the piano was the only real mirror I had then, the only thing that gave me a kind of reality check about how far I'd fallen from the musician my teacher said I could be. The next Ruth Laredo, she'd said. Thank God she couldn't see what had happened to *that* promising girl. I got through the rest of college simply writing papers out of my head often an hour or two before they were due and nodding out most of the rest of the time."

Virginia says she stayed on at college after she graduated because she was offered a job at the music library, a low-paying and virtually clerical job, but at least, she says, "It didn't mean I had to leave or make any decisions for myself." Also working at the library was a sophomore named Kate. "I don't know that I would have noticed Kate except that she was the first human being in my life to notice me—not for being a pianist, which is how I'd gotten most people to notice me, but for what I looked like. She thought I was beautiful and was completely up-front about telling me. It embarrassed me, but it was so tantalizing to be seen as a physical being that it shook me, even through the doped-up haze I was in."

Virginia is slim and tall and had always felt physically awkward. "If I'd ever stood up straight, I'd have measured six-one. But a lifetime of feeling like a complete misfit—which I know had a lot more to do with me internally than externally, but believe me, the height didn't help—it all made me sort of scrunch into myself. I certainly never saw myself as attractive. But Kate did. She said she loved how 'rangy' I was. She was only about five-three and she'd evidently envied tall women all her life. More than envied. I'd already known Kate was lesbian. She was part of the next fraction of a generation who were a little more comfortable, and a little less in-your-face, about being 'out.'

"I'd rather abstractly considered the possibility that I might be lesbian before this, but—maybe because of all the downs I was taking—the thought never really compelled me. Sexually I was just numb; I just wasn't there. I'd experimented with masturbation a little in high school; sounds so clinical, but that's what it was, an experiment. I'd read somewhere about how women should learn to love their bodies and how wonderfully free it made you feel to touch and explore your own body, and I'd always been curious about all this sex stuff that seemed to rivet everybody else. It was mildly pleasant, but I felt silly—ridiculous. I'd never felt comfortable about my big awkward body, and touching it in this self-loving way just somehow made me feel more awkward—and more ugly, somehow, I guess. There was a boy from Amherst who played the oboe, and we'd sometimes play chamber music together with and without other musicians. He was nice to talk to. Two or three times we went to bed with each other. I wasn't turned off, but I wasn't turned on either. To tell you the truth, I was sort of relieved that I wasn't turned on. Maybe the sex part had just been left out of me. It didn't matter. One less thing to worry about. Of course, remember that there wasn't a day when I wasn't what I now realize amounted to semiconscious. It's no wonder I couldn't feel anything sexually. It's a wonder I could feel anything at all. I very nearly couldn't."

But Kate made her feel something. In fact, Kate's attentions had an odd and unusual effect: "They made me sad," Virginia says. "I guess what was happening was that *emotionally* I was being touched in some way I'd never experienced. It was even getting through the blanket of barbiturates. And soon, every time I looked at Kate, who really was a pretty little thing, very 'femme' I guess, soft short blond hair, slight dancer body, I just got sadder. Sometimes even to the point of wanting to cry. I didn't know why, really. I guess I was just so unused to feeling anything for anybody. I don't remember ever even having a crush on anyone when I was a teenager, like every other girl seemed to. It was like I felt, *You're not allowed!* Why I felt like that, I've no idea. My parents are quiet and conservative, but they're not monsters, and they're not undemonstrative with each other. It's not like I grew up in a sex-phobic household.

"Anyway, Kate walked into the storage room one day and saw me standing by the window. I'd been sort of vegging out in my usual way; I suppose I had some books I had to retrieve or put back, I can't remember. But she saw me in front of the window, and she said, 'God, the light's giving your whole body a halo. I wish I could have a picture of you, just like that, standing there. You look so beautiful.' And I burst into tears."

Kate seemed almost to be waiting for the breakdown, Virginia remembers: "She responded so surely—just came over and this little bit of a thing hugged me—hugged my waist, just about. A very soft but very complete embrace, her arms lightly around me. She said little comforting things like, 'It's okay.' It was nearly the end of the day. She offered to walk me home. It was so wonderful feeling her near me. I made a huge effort to pull myself together. I drew myself back and away from her, gently. But I knew I wanted her to walk me home. And she did."

Thus began the first romantic relationship Virginia ever had with a woman, one that virtually instantly erased any doubts about her sexuality. "I don't know that I'd have called myself a lesbian right then. What I felt like was a *Kate*-ian. I didn't suddenly find all women attractive. I found Kate attractive—

irresistible. In fact, I couldn't imagine ever finding anyone else, male or female, attractive. Kate was everything to me. Some door in me just opened with her, and there was room for her and only her inside."

Which is why Virginia was so devastated a week later, when Kate announced that she was pretty sure she couldn't continue to see Virginia unless one thing changed between them. "I freaked out," Virginia said. "There were so many awful things about me. Had Kate been hiding her dislike of one or more of them all this time? Did she hate the fact that I never stood up straight? Maybe—good Lord, I'd never had these thoughts before!—she didn't like how I smelled or the fact that I was so inexperienced as a sexual partner? Or that I didn't talk much? Or said stupid things when I did talk? It was like all the stuff a self-conscious thirteen-year-old girl worries about, all the stuff I had never worried about before because I'd never been in love before. In about forty-five seconds, I'd come up with a mental litany of dozens of my flaws. 'What?' I finally had the courage to ask her."

Virginia says Kate reached out to hold her hand and looked directly into her face, "very gently, but with a very steady strength. In fact, that's what I remember most. It was a little chilling, that strength. Not that she'd suddenly become cold or uncaring to me. I still saw all the love, but it was like it was the first time I saw that she would do whatever she had to do to take care of *herself*. There was this strong autonomy in her. Then she said, 'I can't be around all those pills.'"

## A Delicate Balance

Virginia pauses. "It's funny. You know what's sticking with me now? I mean, of course I can remember what happened next. And in the next few days and weeks and months and years. It changed my life. But now what sticks with me is that word *autonomy*, what I saw in Kate's eyes before she told me she couldn't 'be around all those pills.' It just hit me that I meant something different—or maybe that autonomy means something different to me now than it used to. Until about a minute ago, I probably would have said what I thought scared me back then, the 'chilling' part in Kate's eyes, was that she seemed so *self-sufficient*. Not only determined to take care of herself, but able to. But it's more basic than that. I looked into Kate's eyes and I saw a self. I saw that she *existed*. She knew she took up space; she thought she deserved to take up space. She was really *here*—present—in a way I now, this moment, realize I never ever thought I was. That was what was chilling—the realization that Kate existed and knew she existed and I didn't know what that could possibly feel like. I didn't have a self, as far as I knew. I certainly didn't have a self like Kate did."

Virginia said she needed to cut to the chase, that the point of her story wasn't so much to go over the grim details—trying to make it without her daily dose of downs, which sent her into a state of withdrawal so severe that she had to be hospitalized and treated for depression with more medication; the years of getting off that medication; the incredible support Kate gave her throughout this whole ordeal; the incredible love affair that embraced them but also sometimes brought Virginia to the brink of despair because "it was so hard to let myself be loved"; the relapse Virginia tried to hide when she began to take Valium again; the failed attempts to resume playing the piano; and finally, ten years into her drug-free life, managing to give her first "comeback" recital, with Kate in the audience. And there were Kate's nightmares, which would wake her up, flashbacks to what seemed to Virginia an unbelievably monstrous childhood in which Kate was regularly beaten by her mother who became vicious when she drank, which was virtually every night; Kate's determination never to touch alcohol; and her subsequent addiction to— Virginia wondered why this still surprised her—"pills, just like me!" but uppers as well as downers, with the result that by the age of fifteen she was either comatose or banging off the walls.

"But what I didn't have through almost all of this was a self. That's what I realized right now. And I suppose I just realized it because now I do have a self. That's what just stopped me in my tracks. I think if I looked into my eyes in the mirror right now, I'd see something like what I saw in Kate's eyes way back then. I think I'd see that I was *here*."

Still lovers after twenty years and still obviously in love after all that time, Kate and Virginia have become minor celebrities at their weekly NA meeting, and several women from the group now join them at their house for what Virginia calls "a sort of non-meeting meeting, once a month. I mean, it's not an official NA meeting. It's just basically a bunch of lesbians getting together and trying to make sense of what the hell 'recovery' means. It's like a discussion group, I guess. Maybe Kate and I are the unofficial leaders of it. Everybody seems to be interested in how we managed to stay together so long and like it, how we don't just seem to be disappearing into the relationship in the usual urge-to-merge way. I don't know what they're talking about, really. I mean, I feel like I disappear into Kate all the time. But I guess maybe it is true that I'm *here* now—that I don't erase myself the way I used to."

The discussions can get lively and usually center on whether or not the Twelve Step approach always works for everybody and if it relates to them as gay women. "What makes the group work is that we talk like people, not like placards in a demonstration. I mean, we don't turn into man-hating Marxists or anything. There's no reason to flog the Big Book again and again for its habitual use of the male pronoun. What gets to us more—what certainly gets to me more—is whether the *principles* of the program work to help us stay sober. Whether they're enough—or too much—or might benefit from this or that alteration. In other words, we actually question what seems to make a lot of people in Twelve Step meetings very scared to question. Three women in the group decided not to go to NA or Twelve Step meetings at all for a while; two now go for therapy, and the third goes back to a meeting a few times a year—and they're all still 'clean.' Then one of the women who'd dropped out of NA and found a therapist soon became disenchanted with her therapy and dropped out of that too. She was getting depressed, and the thought of taking drugs was suddenly getting very appealing again. She wanted to know, this last gathering, not as some intellectual exercise but really from the heart, *What did we think recovery meant?* What did sobriety mean? If we said we were sober, what did we mean? Why, really, was it worth pursuing? And how exactly did following the Twelve Step model help us to pursue it—not in some general way, but in each of us individually?"

Virginia says, "We taped this session. We'd never done that before, but Ann, the woman who felt she was on the brink—or as she put it, 'like I've got two choices: throw myself in front of a moving train or start doing cocaine again'—begged us to allow her to tape it so that she could listen to anything she found helpful later on, at home. It was fine with everybody there. We were all friends, and we could see how distraught Ann was. We wanted to help her in whatever way she thought would help. Anyway, this wasn't an NA meeting where we had to worry in any official way about anonymity. So we let her tape it."

Virginia says that Ann later transcribed part of the tape because she wanted Virginia and Kate to see a particular stretch of conversation between them on paper. "It's some of the most interesting stuff about sobriety and recovery I've ever seen," Ann evidently said. "I think you two should read the words you said."

Here's part of that discussion:

V:    Sometimes I wish all the territory *before* you get to the First Step had some steps too. I mean, there's a lot that has to happen before you're ready to "surrender" to an addiction or anything else. And even though I haven't taken a pill in a pretty long time, I always feel like I'm at ground zero with other behaviors. It's like there's no getting away from the chaos and the pain even if you're supposedly sober.

K:    Maybe there's something like a "new addict" or "new alcoholic" these days.

A:    What do you mean?

K:    Well, I was thinking as Virginia was talking that in the sixty or so years since the Big Book was published, people *have* sort of mapped out more territory than the Twelve Steps—we just don't have a second "Big Book" that's collected it all. I don't think the pain of feeling trapped by drugs or booze has changed, or the isolation, or the despair. . . .

V:    Or the ways we lie to ourselves . . .

K:    Yeah, but there is a sort of broader perspective. I mean there have been so many more vocal *women* in recovery, for one thing. And all the issues about sexuality—I don't know. It just seems to me that once you do manage to figure out in some way how to tolerate staying in your own skin, the life you stumble into is so much bigger.

v:    And scarier?

k:    Maybe. But my point is, we know we're so much more than "alcoholics" or "addicts."

a:    That's what gets me sometimes: the fact that *everything* in a Twelve Step meeting is reduced to "staying sober"—which, unless I translate the word "sober" into "alive," just seems so limiting to me. I'm a lot more than a drug addict.

v:    Of course you are. But how a group like NA is set up—well, all it's supposed to be there for is getting sober. And look at us. I mean, we end up talking about a lot more than what drugs we took.

k:    Well, also it's a question of saving your life. I mean, a lot of things can kill you, not just drugs. It seems pretty clear to me, not because Twelve Step dogma or official literature has told me this but because of my own damned experience, that I'd be dead if I hadn't stopped using. Nothing positive would even be possible if I were still using; I understand that this is a "primary" addiction. But *recovery*—well, of course it's a lot bigger than not popping pills.

a:    What are we trying to recover? Sometimes it sounds like getting reupholstered.

v:    I ask myself that a lot. What, after all, am I trying to recover? Not the self I was before I started acting out—that self is what got me into trouble in the first place. What I realize I'm trying to recover is a new capacity for life. A capacity to accept myself across the board. The capacity to love myself and trust that I have the resources to meet whatever life hands me. But also the capacity to reach out for help wherever I could find it—and the capacity to receive help too.

K: I used to go to a therapist when I still drugged; it was a waste of time. . . .

A: I've just been to one, and it's still a waste of time. . . .

V: Yeah, but who really knows what is and what isn't helpful, not now but in the long run? Maybe nothing in my life has been a waste of time: who's to say what was crucial in building up to the moment when I could recover and what wasn't? That period of doped-up analysis may have put a few straws on the camel's back, Kate.

K: I don't know. I only know that one thing is at least possible now that wasn't possible then.

A: What?

K: Finding out who I am, what I'm really like, what I really want. I couldn't know that when I was getting blitzed. There wasn't any room to know it.

V: I think all sobriety really means is *consciousness*. When you're addicted, you're unconscious: you're driven by something deep and hungry, something that blocks any possibility of thought, openness, will, heart, wisdom. I've discovered that anything that increases my consciousness helps me stay—keeps me, if you want to use the other word—"sober." I depend now on a network of friends, like you guys, which helps me on this road to consciousness. I guess I still find my primary help in NA, but, thank God, I'm discovering that the world is infinitely abundant. Everywhere I look I find new resources.

K: Maybe that's what I mean about how there might be a sort of "new" alcoholic or addict these days. The *abundance* of life is the point now, not just the difficulty of staying off drugs or booze.

A: Abundance can feel like chaos.

K: Which is why the Steps still sort of work for me. They're like mileposts, clear guides to what I might want to do instead of freak out in the chaos, or the abundance, or whatever the hell life is.

V: You realize we're not talking, like we usually do, about the difficulties of being female and gay and overlooked by Bill Wilson's heterosexist language?

A: If you'd like, I could resume my scathing critique. . . .

V: Well, that's always fun, and feel free in a moment. But what I was really doing just now was talking to myself. What I was realizing is that, for a moment, I had accepted myself as *human*. I just took it for granted that I'm a human being and I'm alive and I exist and I really don't mind being conscious. Suddenly I didn't have to be "lesbian" or "recovering" or "tall" or a "pianist" or anything specific or limiting to define myself. Something sort of magical happened. I feel like I've got a self.

There was that word again: *self*.

Turning the prism on the Twelve Steps or any other aspect of recovery—as we seem to be unable to keep ourselves from doing—is a sleight-of-hand trick we've had to learn, as gay men and lesbians, not only to make sense of breath mint commercials and sitcoms and most of American culture, but to stay alive. But it does more than offer us a more stereoscopic look at the landscape (both inner and outer) than many other people allow themselves. The wider and more varied our views, in some sense the simpler the finding: *we're* still here. We look into the mirror and we see someone—not a vague amorphous chaotic storm of fear and doubt (which is a pretty good description of what I saw in the mirror on any typical "morning after"), but a self. No matter whether we see the Third Step as a sex aid, a milepost, a nuisance, as easy as art, as hard as algebra, or a part of some ongoing "analysis," the fact we can discover in "sobriety"—in consciousness—*is that somebody is actually doing the seeing.* Somebody's home up there in your head, as well as down there in the jungle of your heart.

The Twelve Step approach is as exasperating or illuminating or as limiting or as freeing as our particular experience of it happens to be at any moment. But what it seems, with a fair degree of consistency, to be giving the people you've just met in this chapter is a home and a schoolroom and an oasis, someplace to sort through the chaos, take a deep breath, and start examining the heart, mind, and soul of the body sitting in your chair. As Ann scribbled at the bottom of the above-quoted transcript: "When I read this, I realize there may really be such a thing as a 'me' after all." Virginia says she flashed back again on the look in Kate's eyes two decades before when she'd said she couldn't be around "all those pills." "There's an even bigger kicker," Virginia said. "There's also a *you*."

Ann, Virginia said, had had another of her cynical moments. "And never the twain shall meet?"

"Oh, I don't know about that," Kate said, walking over to Virginia, standing up on tiptoes before she—very very gently—kissed her sober lover on the chin.

"What Step are you doing now?" Ann asked.

Kate half-whispered her answer: "Every single last one of them."

# 3 Filling Out the Map: Is There Help beyond AA?

In nearly fifteen years of talking with lesbians and gay men who say they're in "recovery"—that is, lesbians and gay men who were able to stop drinking and taking drugs when it became evident that stopping was the only way they had a chance at viable life— I've been looking for common ground, for any singular threads that may unite us. Not only what commonality may exist in the *reasons* so many more of us seem, proportionately, to be alcoholic or drug-addicted than is the case in the "general" population (by some measures one in three for gay people; one in ten for straight people); but what accounted for the many varied routes in recovery I often saw gay people take: routes that often incorporated Twelve Step approaches but that sometimes departed markedly either in their interpretation of those approaches or appended to them vastly different strategies (spiritual, nutritional, "rational," mystical, or psychoanalytic); routes that for some lesbians and gay men have proved to offer strength and guidance in their sober lives.

Actually, identifying some of the external causes for our seemingly rampant addictions didn't, at first, seem so hard. It has long been gay people's own widely shared perception that getting drunk or high was central to being "social" and gay, and for some obvious reasons. Gay culture—at least gay urban culture—has been centrally defined by the gay bar or club; for decades bars were virtually the sole public social venues open to us. Of course, my own experience of being gay and drunk in Vermont (where I went to college and worked for some years after graduating) told me that alcohol was no less a bonding agent for gay people in more rural climes. In fact, if anything, parties held at private houses up in the Green Mountains were more sodden with alcohol and drugs than they were at bars for the simple reason that we could get more blitzed because we didn't have to go anywhere. You could continue drinking, pass out on the floor, or have sex in the nearest bedroom long past whatever hour bars would have closed. There were also often fewer restrictions in somebody's home than there would have been at a gay watering hole, assuming there'd been one to go to.

The way we've made getting high a condition for having "fun" is a red flag to me, a sign that we're fighting some formidable inner demons: often crippling shame and fear about who we are not only as sexual beings but as people. We so often resort to alcohol and drugs because they're such effective superego solvents; they dissolve the nay-saying conscience; they lessen if not eradicate inhibitions. They let us, in other words, do what we "want" to do, a freedom many of us couldn't conceive except under the influence. For many of us, sex was the big prize that these "solvents" alone made possible: remember Stan's startling discovery that just about every "Hick Homo" on the Internet couldn't imagine "doing it" without getting high? With the guilt temporarily blasted out of us by booze and drugs, we could feel—at least for moments—as close to full, free, thoughtless self-acceptance as we could manage. Like kids told for their whole lives not to do something "bad," we fled straight for the taboo when we were high or smashed enough not to care about the social censure (and internal self-censure) we risked by fleeing to it.

The payoffs of getting high have long been clear to us, and in many ways they still apply: we are still arguably a bar or drug culture for some of the same reasons we sniffed ethyl chloride in the 1970s, drank absinthe in the 1890s, or got blitzed on London gin in the 1660s. However, that the sole purpose of alcohol and drugs is to afford us escape strikes many recovering gay men and women I've spoken with as insufficient explanation. As an ostracized group (and we are, of course, *still* an ostracized group, despite whatever cultural or legislative advances we can claim), we would quite naturally seek to escape any society that shuns us or any uncomfortable notions within ourselves that tell us we're sick or evil. But many of us know that we are also *seeking* something in this escape, even if we may be only vaguely aware what we want that "something" to be—love, a tolerable identity, some sense of community, some at least nascent sense that we're not the pariahs we've been told (and we tell ourselves) we are. Alcohol and other drugs not only provide us an escape *from*, but they are also at least an attempted journey *to*, a seeking after something new and better and more fulfilling. In the end, our motives to drink and drug may not be so much to get away from who we are as to rush to some new vision of who we are that we can tolerate—a vision that allows us to be fully and unimpededly physical, emotional, loving, sexual, and spiritual beings.

Carl Jung's famous observation in his letter to Bill Wilson that alcohol is *spiritus* in Latin and that *spiritus* describes both the most depraving poison (alcohol) as well as the highest reaches of the soul describes the heart of an observation I have heard many gay women and men voice too. Many of us readily recognize that there's a kind of "soul hunger" fueling our addictive behaviors. In fact, every recovering gay woman or man with whom I've spoken nods a vigorous YES at hearing the news that what they really were after when they drank or drugged wasn't simply conscience-free sexual license, but a more basic freedom of self—of *soul*. In the same way, the phrase "soul sickness" is instantly comprehensible to gay men and women in recovery, even those for whom "soul" is merely a metaphor for something like "psyche" or "personality."

Iconoclasts in recovery—those who find help "beyond" the Twelve Steps—do seem to me to have accommodated themselves, in ways that make sense to them, to the principles of Twelve Step recovery, importantly including a sense of "surrender" to the substance or behavior that reflexively turns them into self-destructive robots, the realization that they cannot battle their addictions alone, and a growing sense of something fueling their recovery that is larger than their own fallible wills, even if they may resist defining these principles in the terms provided by the First, Second, or Third Steps.

Indeed, most gay men and women I know who've been sober for longer than two or three years have either added to their Twelve Step experience a variety of other approaches or interpreted the program in idiosyncratic ways that make particular sense to them. Lesbians and gay men vividly give evidence that no system of achieving sobriety can work if you don't make it your own: it can't make sense in some abstract way; it has to make sense to *you*. They also make it clear that not all sobriety is forged exclusively in AA. In Bill Wilson's manifesto, colloquially dubbed the Big Book (*Alcoholics Anonymous*), Bill tells us of his own pre-AA search for relief from his alcoholism—everything from spa cures to psychoanalysis—and he gives each approach its due. His revelation that recovery from alcoholism was essentially spiritual had many philosophical roots, most notably (as Nan Robertson, in her excellent history of Alcoholics Anonymous, *Getting Better*, tells us) in the largely Christian Oxford Movement of the 1920s and 1930s. Wilson's curiosity about exploring numerous routes to self-realization in sobriety never ceased throughout his life (even including some experiments with LSD in the 1960s). The road to a life that was "happy, joyous and free" is long and broad; it beckons us, once again, to cultivate our own revelations and curiosities about conscious, sober life. Some of the most inspiring and refreshing voices I've heard about this journey toward consciousness come from what staunch Twelve-Steppers might think of warily as the disenfranchised—people who may attend this or that Twelve Step meeting to "touch base," but who put a good deal of energy into other means of staying sober and enhancing conscious life as well.

I love AA and I love the wisdom of the Twelve Step approach: it saved my life, and elements of it continue to save my life today. In fact, as I've suggested, the essential elements of it can be found (I believe) in any method of attaining and maintaining sobriety, no matter how wary its adherents may be about AA. But the fact remains that not all of us seek guidance and recovery soley from Twelve Step programs. Recovering gay men and lesbians are often the most prominent pioneers in widening our sense of what sobriety can mean and how to achieve and sustain it.

I began by saying I've always sought common threads that may unite all these different takes and approaches—not only those that may unite gay people in their experience of addiction and recovery, but also those that may clarify what *makes any method of recovery work*. We've already begun to see some particles of that thread: Honesty—starting with self-honesty. Connection—the feeling that we are not unreachably alone in the universe. Support—surrounding ourselves with some sort of embracing, even cheerleading, "family" of people who love us, want the best for us, and are willing to do what they can to help us to renew our pacts not to drink or drug; to help us, in other words, keep to our pacts not to kill ourselves. But is there another part of this thread?

I believe there is: not only our hunger for a kind of "spiritual" completion, but our experience of what that spiritual gratification feels like and is. It strikes me that what most gay men and lesbians mean by the word "spirituality" seems to change as we forge further into recovery. Full sober pleasure turns out not to be something as simple or monochromatic as a chemically induced high. It's more than any simple release. Conscious pleasure engages the whole psyche: dark as well as light, it draws as much from sadness as elation, connecting us to others not isolating us in some impenetrable altered state. It includes; it doesn't exclude. It has chiaroscuro, shading, three dimensions. Once again, it is a movement *to*, not an escape *from*. For lesbians and gay men, true spirituality does something Bill Wilson never explicitly named: it heals the wounds caused by our own internalized homophobia. It makes us, in very particular ways, far more deeply self-accepting as gay men and lesbians.

There is always danger, of course. Our deepest motives, as Jung suggested to Bill Wilson, may collectively be to achieve freedom of self (*spiritus* as soul), but our hunger for this freedom is sometimes so urgent that we never get past gratifying the body and ego (*spiritus* as booze or drugs). Relapse is a big problem for gay men and lesbians partly because of this impatience for a concrete, immediate reward. But when we experience the miracle of surrender (in whatever terms we choose to define it) and begin on our individual roads to recovery, we learn that we can continue to make use of the same urgent hunger for release we've always felt—only now our yearning for *enjoyment* in life saves rather than stymies us: it can turn into a guide, not a killer.

Because we know how liberating the most transcendent, soul-affirming pleasure can be, we're usually phenomenally sensitive to (so that we can defend against) its opposites—phobia and bigotry—however subtly disguised, however well-meaning the conscious motives clothing them. We are typically suspicious whenever groups form and make unilateral pronouncements, whether it's the Ku Klux Klan, the DAR, Act Up, or even AA. We tend so quickly to see the phobic mob instinct behind the most allegedly foregone truths—for example, "protecting your children against unsavory influences" (namely, their gay third-grade teacher)—because we are attuned even to the most hidden ulterior motives; second-guessing them to fend them off is a tactic most of us have depended on to survive. Thus a lot of us aren't crazy about groups and Groupspeak. To wit:

"I hate groups, I hate God-talk, I hate sloganeering, and I'm especially wary of the mob instinct that seems to describe a lot of people I've known who've clung to AA and NA as if it were something handed down by Moses," says Arianne, an advertising executive in Washington who, at thirty-six, has been sober "mostly on my own" for ten years. "As much as I hear that Twelve Step programs are supposed to be nonevangelical—they work by the power of example—almost everyone I know who goes to AA is an out-and-out evangelist. And as far as making you 'happy, joyous and free'—well, too many AA people I've met seem far from that, even if, endlessly, they tell me different."

Arianne also has problems with the language of AA literature, which seems to her inescapably sexist. "I get tired of having to translate all the time. I mean, it's taken for granted throughout so much of the Big Book that men work, women stay home, and everyone is heterosexual. I know this is a product of Bill Wilson's time and culture, but it's still alienating. This coupled with the religious-sounding language has sometimes turned me off big time."

What does work for her? "Well, it started with something simple," she says. "I got sick of killing myself. It really isn't more complicated than that. I came to the realization that I didn't want to die of cirrhosis of the liver, which was the destination I was definitely moving toward when I drank. I was so enmeshed in the lesbian bar scene—God, it's such a myth that gay women aren't naturally promiscuous. I was sleeping around with every woman I could get my hands on. And I don't think I ever had sex when I wasn't drunk. It got so out of hand that after a while I just came to a dead halt. I couldn't stand my life anymore. Something in me said to stop killing myself. I guess an AA-er would call it a 'spiritual awakening,' but to me it was just resounding common sense. I don't believe in God. I do, however, believe, from the therapy I've been in, that we're propelled by immensely strong urges. I like Freud's idea that they're divided into life and death. Yeah, I know it's not p.c. to like Freud if you're a lesbian—or even a woman. But those drives Freud talked about make a good metaphor for me; it strikes me as true. I think so much of human life and motivation is a matter of individual temperament. And my temperament turned out to be a little stronger on the life side than on the death side. Once I realized I wanted to live, I stopped drinking."

Did she look to others for support? "Well, at the beginning, if you'd asked me that, I think I would have said no," Arianne says. "I did pretty quickly start in analysis after I stopped drinking, but not right after. I was lucky, I guess. Stopping this mode of suicide was such a physical relief to me. I just felt better. Then my curiosity clicked in. I wanted to know more about myself. I guess because my 'self' was more consciously evident to me. So I started going to a shrink a friend of mine recommended. And that started out being my main means of 'support,' I suppose. But while it felt like a lone journey at first, although a journey every step of which I reported to my analyst, slowly the circle of people I talked with widened. The more I learned about myself and the more I could accept my fallibilities, the more I could accept other people's. I even started going to some AA meetings. I lost some of the chip on my shoulder, I guess.

"But I think my greatest fear was that life would just be boring without getting high, no matter who else I talked to about it. It turns out I was wrong. Sobriety is exasperating, sometimes—unnerving in the clarity it gives me—but it sure isn't boring. The adventure just continues, and deepens. I don't want to turn back from it anymore. I've discovered I can come out of even the scariest moments with new illumination. Am I 'happy'? I don't know. Sometimes. Am I 'alive'? Without a doubt, yes."

*It sure isn't boring. . . . The adventure just continues, and deepens.* Alive seems better than happy to Arianne, because to be fully alive is to experience life more completely—and in a sense more richly, pleasurably—than any glazed-over, lambs-leaping-in-May "happy" state could ever provide. "Spare me that kind of happiness, which just strikes me as one more way of being drunk!" Arianne says. "Give me *life*. It's *that* sense of ground-to-heaven pleasure I've learned to seek more consciously. It's strange what's helped me as I've gone on. Not only my analysis, not only going to AA meetings, but also delving into certain meditative and religious practices based on matriarchy, close to 'witchcraft' in some people's minds, I guess—approaches to spirituality that celebrate various notions of goddess, of a kind of maternal spirit that runs through all things. I started going to lesbian groups that explored this, and met women who—surprisingly, to me—also went to AA. Slowly, especially as I went with my new friends to AA meetings, some of which were women only and filled with lesbians who expressed a great deal more anger about sexist assumptions even than I had, I began to feel less defensive and angry about Twelve Step language. More important, I could see so many connections—both in terms of pragmatic decisions (like not walking home from work past my old bar) and in terms of the kind of spiritual exploration I was making in my coven of witches, in people who I began to realize were after the same feeling of freedom and release I craved. I guess I don't feel I have to lash out so much anymore. The idea of taking what works and leaving the rest—something in me has eased about all this. All of the ways I connect with other people constitute a kind of mix-and-match strategy that works, something that feeds my soul as much as it helps me get through day-to-day life. I haven't picked up a drink today, which is my proof that it's working."

Arianne first saw her alcoholism in practical terms. She had a choice: cirrhosis of the liver or abstinence from booze. This practical reality was enough for her (as, of course, it isn't always for other people) to get her to stop drinking and stay stopped, at least initially. Other recovering gay people I've talked to have found strength in changing their nutritional and exercise habits, as well as through psychotherapy. Others may have started out in Twelve Step programs but quite honestly questioned various aspects of them, especially the fearful or dogmatic dire warnings expressed by some people at meetings that if you didn't do it "the right way," you'd die.

But certain bedrock conditions common to every long-term recoverer still in various ways seem to prevail: for example, not feeling alone. While Arianne once scoffed at the idea that she needed anyone else to keep her sober, she's now clear that the journey she is on does involve other people, starting with her therapist, widening to include her witches and recovering lesbian sisters. She feels connected not only to her therapist but viscerally to the adventure of life in sobriety in ways she never had before. And she's receptive to support in ways she never was receptive before.

Every story I've so far recounted is in some way a story of how, idiosyncratically, each recovering man or woman met these seemingly essential conditions for sobriety or recovery, even if their means of meeting them might sometimes have made the hairs on Bill Wilson's neck stand up.

For example, Adam.

## Paying Attention to Compulsion: Adam's Tale

"First of all, let me clear one thing up about the man you see in front of you right now." (The man I saw before me, Adam—black, golden-eyed, tall, muscular, gloriously handsome—was quite a man to see.) "Whatever light or life you see is coming from pure unadulterated me. I haven't done any drugs—it amazes me when I think of it—for over a year. But, okay, I'll tell you the story about How Adam Stopped Using.

"First of all, what I got hooked on was crystal meth, with little side doses of 'Special κ.' These are really seductive drugs, and they're widely used and abused by gay men. They make you feel sexual, and if you devise the right combination, they don't turn you into a drooling idiot or a paranoid maniac—well, at least not at first. But eventually, like some kind of slow-acting corrosive acid, they eat away at you inside until you feel like a hollow shell. They also bankrupt you. They're expensive, especially on the East Coast. However, I didn't stop only because I couldn't pay my rent. That makes it sound too practical. Actually the trigger reason was simpler.

"Jamie, who was one of my fuckbuddies—my life had been full of an overlapping series of them, and up until then it seemed to suit my temperament just fine—anyway, Jamie told me about this chakra worker he'd started going to, and now went to all the time, and how wonderful the experience was. What intrigued me wasn't the chakra business—I mean, I usually groan at all that New Age voodoo stuff. What intrigued me is that my friend, who was as sophisticated a drug user as I was, and with whom I had scenes that lasted thirty-nine nonstop hours because of the extraordinary way crystal meth and Special κ kept us both bonded and focused and capable of better sex than I ever thought a human being could have—anyway, what intrigued me is that my friend stopped doing drugs. And there was a difference, but it wasn't the difference I expected. There was something a little more, I don't know how to say it, *childlike* about him, more yielding when I held him. He was like, in some way, he was softer—inside, not outside! In fact, that was another thing, the outside. Crystal generally kills erections for the first long stretch, and that stretch can last a lot of hours. Of course, on crystal—Californians call this shit 'crank'—you don't need an erection to feel erotic. But I guess what I'm trying to say is that something about Jamie got more interesting and exciting, not less, after he stopped drugs. And that's what intrigued me. It was almost as if he had found another drug, a substitute that was vastly more than the thing whose place it took. [Irresistible aside: Adam said these words before he or I had a clue what the title of this book would be, and, believe me, he was no scholar of the Big Book.] Who wouldn't want to try something like that?"

Adam shrugged. "Of course, it helped that going to this chakra worker was cheap as well. By now, like I said, my crystal-and-K cocktails were bankrupting me. I'd worked freelance for legal and advertising and publishing companies doing word processing and once was making some pretty good money as a one-man consultancy firm. But the jobs started to bore me so much, I just couldn't bring myself to get them done anywhere near on time. One after another, clients dropped me. Then, like I said, I decided to hustle every so often, which, over the sex phone lines in New York, was easy enough to do. I even got myself a beeper. That all worked okay, until I realized that it wasn't enough sexually for me to be adored—which is pretty much what happened when the overweight closeted fifty-year-old businessmen who were my main clientele sheepishly met me at their hotel room doors and fell to their knees. I didn't want to have sex that wasn't good, even if I got paid for it. And I got paid better than they realized they were paying me. Open wallets were a magnet to me. I was hustling and stealing and, somehow, not enjoying any of it very much. The money kept draining away as well as the pleasure. Something in the center of me was draining away. I was really, totally—for the first time in my life—completely miserable."

So Adam says he tried out the chakra worker.

First of all, the chakra worker was not, as Adam was sure he would be, a sweet lithe androgynous dreamy-eyed overaged hippie. He was a she. Her name (which Adam said turned out to be almost overkill-appropriate) was Grace. "She's the sort of woman you'd expect to see behind the hot lunch counter at an elementary school. Plump and placid. I don't know what mixture of ethnicities she was—there seemed to be a little Filipino, a little African, a little Mexican. Funny how I haven't gotten around to asking her about any of that. It just never seemed to matter. But the effect was, she was somehow 'Everyone.' It's like God had taken drops from all the bottles of human essences on his shelf and poured them all into Grace. I don't mean to make her sound like Mother Teresa or someone. Grace just came across as sweet and maternal when you met her, not some tirelessly selfless saint. She loved to eat. She'd always have incredible little cookies and savory crackers and bowls of amazing morsels of food: she baked them like they were little pieces of sculpture you ate instead of looked at. There wasn't a thing in the world you couldn't tell her. None of whatever came out of your mouth made much difference to her. What she was interested in was your body, and I'll never forget what she said when she first saw my body. Not because I'd never heard the words before—I'd heard them on the average of six times a day. But because I'd never *understood* them like I did when Grace said them.

"'You're beautiful.' That's what she said. I don't remember any other words that passed between us that first session. The revelation was simply this: I knew that she was saying something different from 'You've got a beautiful butt or chest or dick.' It was the first time I encountered the full possibility of a different kind of beauty. It's not just a question of external and internal. No, what Grace was talking about—I now know—was something that encompassed both, was greater than both. God, the New Age-isms are hard to resist, but it's hard to find words for this."

Not, Adam says, that Grace did anything to him that first session particularly unusual. "In fact, if anything I was a little disappointed in the physical part. She simply massaged me—conventionally, kneading my shoulders, back, neck, arms, butt, and the rest of me. It felt nice, but it wasn't anything especially mind-altering. The only difference from a regular health-club-type massage and Grace's massage was that she paused longer between parts of the body. Like she'd work my shoulders rhythmically with her hands and begin to go down my back, and then she'd stop. I don't know what she did in these silences. I think she was simply looking at me. This would last maybe ten seconds; then she'd start kneading my back in the conventional way. Then she proceeded similarly—stop and go—until she'd touched every part of me, although modestly avoiding the genitalia, and then she said she was done."

Adam says he asked her what her diagnosis was. Grace looked at him mildly and said she'd have to think about it but next week, when he came back, they'd sit and talk, and she'd probably have something to say about it then. "This seemed awfully laid back, but hey, I was ready to give her a chance. The following week didn't have any earth-shattering significance to me, although I did keep remembering her tone when she'd said 'you're beautiful,' trying to figure out why it seemed it was the first time I'd heard those words. The following week I went back and she sat me down and offered me her latest bowl of cheese garlic basil salsa chips (you have never tasted anything like them) and took out a beaten, often folded and unfolded poster of a body—a female body!—with its chakras marked in the usual places. She apologized for not being able to find the chart with the male body, but she said it didn't really matter. I remember thinking: at least the food is good! I mean, I really was not expecting to hear anything profound from this mild maternal masseuse. Maybe Jamie had some particular mother fixation and that's why he found Grace so life-changing?"

Grace began. "I'm gay too," she said, a little shyly.

Adam said he was delighted to hear it.

"I used to have a lover. She died. Of breast cancer. That was six years ago. There's really not room for anyone else in my heart. Not like that."

Adam offered his condolences.

Grace then pointed to the female outline in the chart. "She taught me about the chakras." Grace pronounced the word lovingly, with a soft "ch." "This is where they are," she said, pointing first to the base of the cartoon's spine, then the crotch, the pit of the stomach, chest, throat, forehead, and the very top of the head. "There are seven of them. I wrote down the words they mean for you to take home with you." Adam looked down to see a careful, almost Catholic-girls'-school handwriting—blue Bic pen ink pressed hard into the lined paper. The words were Security, Passion and Sensation, Power, Love, Communication, Perception, and Wisdom. "The one you have to look out for is Love. The chest. You are perfectly fine in every other one." She sat back, evidently done with all she had planned to say. Adam says he looked at her expectantly anyway. Grace smiled back at him.

"Would you like another massage?" she asked him. Adam said sure, that would be nice. "Some instinct told me to keep the 3,068 questions that were buzzing in my head to myself. I was going to do nothing but whatever seemed simplest. I still harbored the idea that this was one hell of an overrated chakra worker—what could Jamie have been talking about, this nirvana she'd brought him to? But something in that sweet bland face told me that perhaps the empress *was* wearing a beautiful robe I couldn't yet see. Anyway, she was a competent enough masseuse. So I stripped again and she looked at me appreciatively again and she gave me a repeat of the previous week's rubdown, although this time pausing for less time between each area of the body and taking a little bit longer with my pecs. When I closed my eyes, all I could see for the longest while was the list of carefully penned words she'd shown me. I saw the curlicued L on the Love one, the chest one, the one she said I had to pay attention to. I sort of saw my own nicely muscled chest peeping through the lined paper, as if the paper weren't paper anymore but gauze. I could see the outline of my own torso as she worked away on me. . . ."

Adam felt a little more fundamentally different at the end of this session than he had at the first. When she was done and he opened his eyes and once again saw the handwritten list she was giving him, he saw she'd underlined the middle one, Love—an underscoring that hadn't been there the last time he'd looked at the page. She observed his gaze at the paper. "You can ask me anything you like, you know," she said. And Adam wondered what he could possibly ask. Not that he didn't have questions, but they weren't the quippy ones that had been buzzing in his head before. It was something more amorphous, gauzy, less articulate— something that felt like an ache rather than a question he could put into words. The only thing he could think of to say was, "Is there anything I should be doing?"

Grace screwed up her face into such an intense frown of hard thought that Adam almost laughed. "It was the sort of expression you'd expect to precede her giving me her most complicated cheese-chip recipe, the one with the truffle-and-chipotle sauce. Then her brow cleared. 'Well,' she said, 'you might look at the list once or twice.' She seemed satisfied. And the weird thing was, I was satisfied. It seemed somehow the perfect thing to say, the thing I'd been waiting all my life to hear."

Adam says he retained this feeling of completeness—this feeling somehow of knowing what he had to do—on the whole half-hour subway ride back to his apartment. "When I got back home, though, I started to pick away at the feeling. Boy, I thought I was a master at mind-fucking. This lady was like Machiavelli at it. Or was she just a simple-minded sweet lesbian cookie-baker? Was I making all this up? What was happening to me? Why did I feel different? And why—this was the biggest kick in the butt—didn't I feel like doing any drugs that night?"

Now, over a year later, Adam is more sure about what was going on then, and he's tentatively articulate about what he's going through now: his version of "uncovery." "It's like, all she had to say to me were the words 'Heart' and 'Love.' My own blasting crazy free-associating mind would do the rest. Grace knew that. She even said it. Don't think I've never asked her questions—now I ask them all the time. In fact, the first real question I asked her was the next week. I said, 'Why do I feel better?' That seemed like it would cut to the chase quickest. She understood the question completely. 'I knew you had all this energy in your head and that you could talk forever about anything and everything whenever you wanted to. I could hear all that sound. It was a wonderful sound, like this orchestra playing full blast all the time. What would I have to say to an orchestra already playing its beautiful music? I had no things to tell it; it was too busy telling me what it wanted to say. But you know how sometimes you hear a band or an orchestra and you think, I wish the bass drum would beat a little louder; I can't hear it as much as I'd like to? Well, that's what I was doing when I said you had to pay attention to your heart. I wanted to hear more of the bass drum—more of that big happy *boom!* But I didn't have to tell you that. You knew that on your own. You're a very experienced orchestra conductor! Much better at what you do than I could ever be.'"

I asked her a second question. "Why don't I want to get high anymore?"

Grace responded as if she'd known the answer to this one all her life—like why she'd left out the red pepper in her simplest recipe. "Because you see now that it gets in the way."

This sank in, Adam says, "like rain on the desert. That's exactly the change I hadn't been able to put words to. Some new feeling was growing at a surprisingly quick rate, and it was growing right in the middle of my chest, filling it up. The more I felt it, the less I even had the inclination to think of getting high. It wasn't like I said to myself, 'Thank God, you're not addicted anymore!' I'd never especially thought of myself as addicted to begin with, at least not back then. What I thought was, 'Thank God, I can feel a whole new kind of pleasure without consuming any drug to create it!' I was moving from one feeling to a more satisfying one. I was moving toward pleasure, not away from it."

Adam was so delighted with this revelation because it seemed the last little piece in his jigsaw puzzle—it seemed, in other words, like the great dilemma of Life had been solved forever. "It was like I felt this boundless *resource* in the center of me. I began to see Jamie a little more often, although not for the marathon sessions we'd had before. Crystal turned out to be the thing that enabled marathons to happen, and neither one of us was doing crystal anymore. The lovemaking was gentle and amazing and powerful. I really thought, *Now I can get on with my life*. Now there will be no more conflict—there's no *need* for any conflict. Ask me the Secret of the Universe—go ahead. I'm ready. . . .

"Until one morning, the day before I was to see Grace again— before, I think, my sixth or seventh session with her—I woke up in a terrible cold sweat. I felt the most excruciating anguish I had ever felt in my life. And I had no idea where it was coming from. It was like lava erupting into the center of me, right into my heart. All these childhood memories came back—as much as I'd defended my mother, all those bleak long afternoons alone in the kitchen with my dad on rainy Saturdays flooded back in, both of us silent about our secret suspicion that Mom wasn't just on a shopping jaunt in Manhattan, that she had left us more com- pletely than that, that there was somebody else she loved more than us. And looking at my father and seeing how shut down he was, how sad and despairing he was, how much I wanted to hug him, but how distant and cold and unreceptive he always was to me. How I had nothing to talk to him about. How it was as if, with Mom gone and him basically 'gone' in his head, I was alone in that cold kitchen. Alone and very hungry and nobody to feed me. The taste of Grace's savory chips exploded in my mouth, and I started to cry. Sob. Howl."

Adam promptly got some crystal meth and went to Grace's the next day high on it, having stayed awake the entire preceding night because of it. Grace smiled at him as usual, seemingly un- surprised when he turned down her offer of what had been his fa- vorite bowl of hot peppered Grace-food (crystal kills the appetite as well as erections, Adam reminded me) and gave him her usual competent massage, though perhaps pausing a bit longer than she'd done recently between body parts. "I'm on crystal again," he told her needlessly. Adam had already known she knew this. Grace said yes, she hoped I was enjoying myself, and then finished her massage. She said, "See you next week" as she always did, and Adam left.

When he got home, he took the little blue glassine packet in his medicine cabinet out and threw its tiny sparkling contents down the toilet.

"I don't know what to tell you, really, besides that," he said, as enigmatic, probably, as Grace had ever been. "Except maybe this: I don't want anything to get in the way again. Of any feeling. Shortly after I had that toxic eruption, I actually started going to some NA meetings; I was curious about this thing called 'compulsion.' What did it really mean, my feeling compelled to search for pleasure in the ways I did? I felt receptive to anyone who had an opinion when I started out. I felt like suddenly I knew so little, and it was time to listen. But the problem with many of the Twelve Step meetings I went to is that they seemed too fear-ridden—sort of strident, desperate. They didn't always give me what I needed, somehow. It was a problem more of tone than content. I guess Grace had the right tone for me, and that's what makes her brand of whatever it is she does work for me.

"One thing I know from all this is that there's as much toxic rage and hate in me as there is love and elation. That's what I realized, I guess, when I threw that crystal away, that something incredibly wonderful happened when I let out whatever I was feeling, however intensely I was feeling it, and however horrible it was—let it out directly, right then and there, and hung on for the ride. It's like a periodic cleaning out. That's all. It's sort of my psyche maintaining itself, doing what it has to do to keep its health and get what it needs. And the weird thing is, one of the net results seems to be a better handle on 'shared reality.' I mean, I feel more able now to get work done on time. My clients are starting to come back to me. I'm sort of connecting to people in a different way. Jamie is almost even turning into a lover—at least, I want to see him now not just for sex, but to be with him. To sort of be *Grace* with him—not talk, just be, and maybe take a glance at Grace's chakra list, which is now framed and in prominent view on my living room wall. It's not so much that anything about me has changed; it's that who I am, who I've always been, who I'm becoming, is coming out unimpeded. And that's what's saving my butt, I guess. And making me feel like I actually might love Jamie, not just lust after him. I used to think that love was a pretty wimpy substitute for lust. It's what people said when they lost interest in somebody sexually but didn't want to hurt their feelings. Doesn't seem true to me anymore."

Adam looks almost sheepish about what he obviously wants to say next. "Another thing's changed. I *care* more. Not just about me. Not just about how well I can manipulate people. But I actually care more about—well, not just Jamie, but my clients. For instance, this middle-aged hard-ass lawyer who uses me to prepare all her briefs called me a couple weeks ago. She's always so clipped and businesslike when she talks to me, but this time, her voice was trembling a little. Turned out her sister had just died of cancer. It was her twin sister. They hadn't seen each other in three years, because she lived on the other side of the country. She was devastated. I'd never heard her sound so vulnerable before, like a little girl. While she was calling me for a business reason, to ask me if I could finish the work she'd given me a week early, I asked her if there was anything I could do. She paused for a moment, and I swear I heard something like a stifled sob—she probably covered the phone speaker with her hand. 'I have nobody to take care of my cats when I go to the funeral. You don't know anybody who could . . .' And I volunteered to do it myself. Man, I used to pride myself on being a selfish black sonovabitch, and here I was helping this tight-assed lawyer. But, well, it's not the first time stuff like this has happened. It's like, somehow, I just damned *care* more. I don't especially want to. I just do. So maybe that has something to do with Grace and quitting crystal and all the rest of it."

There is a softening process in "sobriety." We yield in ways that frequently surprise us: they seem so unlike the "old" selves we were. Adam didn't start caring as the result of any imposed "service" (of the kind that AA encourages, from acting as sponsor to making the coffee or setting up the chairs at an AA meeting); it was as natural a product of his recovery as his newfound ability to hold on to his clients, meet his deadlines, and begin to see Jamie as a lover, not merely a fuckbuddy.

But Adam makes vivid for me another perhaps more revolutionary idea, as well: that "compulsive behavior" is not ultimately what we so often hear that it is from recovery pundits in meetings or books or textbooks on alcoholism—"self-destructive" in its motive. It may result in behavior that breaks down the body, soul, emotions, mind, and psyche, but its motive is not self-destructive at all. I remind myself again of Jung's dual interpretation of *spiritus*: whether we're pursuing crystal meth or vodka or marijuana, or a "happy, joyous and free" life in sobriety, our motive is to move us toward the most exquisitely gratifying experience of life we can find. I've suggested why so many gay people feel this blindingly powerful urge for pleasure more than others: it's a reaction to our profound experience of deprivation, *being deprived of selfhood*—a sense of existential rejection that usually dates back to the first early childhood moments when we learned that who we were most primally was contemptible. But maybe it's more mysterious than this. Adam tells me it's a question Grace wouldn't even try to answer, except with the most banal cliché of common sense: "Some people are just born that way, I guess."

But the pursuit of this joy in life does seem to be the motive behind both our addictions *and* (in strange new ways) our recoveries—even if it seems, especially for those gay men and women I've spoken to who crave the most encompassing and ultimate and profound and transcendent pleasures they can find, that "pleasure" has a very different and much stranger meaning than we may have started thinking.

"It's not the pleasure of an orgasm anymore," Adam says. "It's the pleasure of feeling fully alive. I wish there were a sharper way to say it. But basically, I don't want to stop with a good meal or a good paycheck or a good roll in the hay, much as I love all that. I want something much more. And my sessions with Grace—maybe more how I reflect on those sessions after they happen—are teaching me that I can get that 'more' by getting *clear*. Why put boulders in the road when you're about to break a speed record? Just get out of your own way. I know everyone from here to Marin County's been saying that since about 1965, but . . . well, I don't know how else to put it. Although I did say this the other day to somebody else who asked me what he should do to quit taking drugs. 'Be yourself' is all I could think of to say. Then I gave him Grace's phone number."

"Be yourself" may sound awfully dangerous; didn't we get into trouble by "being ourselves"? Adam explains: "Actually, my recovery now is in some ways counterintuitive. I mean, my 'intuition' is still often that I need to escape in the old ways—according to the old, fearful self I was; sometimes the only hope at all seems to lie in crystal and sex and manipulating the world in the old ways. But I know now that that's not the real me, that's the fearful me. The real me is larger than that fearful child scurrying to his next quick fix. And here's where the Twelve Step idea of surrender and seeking help in a Higher Power does make very strong good sense to me. I know I'm my larger 'true' self when I'm able to feel that surrender. I know I'm not that self when my

instincts tell me to hide and lie low and connive my way to grabbing some quick palliative. It's a bigger, larger game than I realized, and I don't have to be afraid."

When we can step back from it, we often see a very clear message in our own compulsive urges and pasts (and presents): we see
our cravings writ large and bold across the sky, like the Wicked
Witch's white-smoke "SURRENDER DOROTHY" over Oz. We see
the pure howl of our cravings for a kind of *oneness* within our lives
and with other people. As you'll see, I think, even more clearly
later on in these pages, our "compulsions" are the source of so
much information about what we most dearly and specifically
want in our lives. They tell us in the clearest ways possible what
we should pursue—what we need to pursue, not what we should
avoid. This is why analyzing our past and present behavior in
terms of compulsivity (as we're beckoned to do in AA's Fourth
and Tenth Steps) is so important: by paying attention to what
compels us, we become far more acquainted with *what we really
want*. It turns out, as Adam and Arianne have discovered, that
their prospects of actually getting what they want increase geo-
metrically in sobriety—something you couldn't have convinced
either of them back when they were drinking or drugging.

The trick, of course, is learning that paying attention to compulsion doesn't mean always acting on it in the same ways. What
our psyches compel us to find, to consume, to immerse ourselves
in can be found and consumed in a variety of ways, ways that
don't have to kill us physically, spiritually, or mentally. Adam says
that while he himself has a good deal of resistance to the structure and implementation of Twelve Step programs, he once saw
Grace at an NA meeting. "I was surprised and asked her why she'd
come. Surely *she* didn't need to go to meetings! She gave me her
usual hot lunch lady smile and said, 'Oh, I come here all the time.
I like to hear the people talk. I learn so much.'

"Go figure," Adam shrugs, laughing. Then he starts to sing the opening lines of the hymn with which he now associates her: "Amazing Grace, how sweet the sound . . ." A state of grace, a gift, a momentary reprieve: the "now" quality of sobriety is what strikes Adam most. "Grace and I go to meetings all the time now," he says. "Somehow, sitting next to her, I'm just not so bothered by the fear and dogma and constrained language anymore. I'm starting to see and hear so much else in 'the rooms' than I could allow myself to hear before."

## The Joy of Being Silly

When I told Lorie about Adam's experience with Grace, she shuddered. "Oh boy," she said. "I need a whole lot more than some plump lady guru smiling at me like Mona Lisa to keep me from the bourbon bottle." Like AA? "Oh, I go to meetings, especially when I can drive into Chicago and go to a gay and lesbian one. But that's not only what does it for me." What does?

Lorie says it simply: "Being rational." Lorie didn't mean this solely in the commonsense way that Arianne used the word. She was and is a proponent of the "rational therapy" approach to alcoholism, based on tenets of Albert Ellis's rational-emotive therapy—an approach that invites you to question (and generally laugh hysterically at) the absurdity of the assumptions behind behavior you may think is serving you, but in fact is sabotaging you.

The child of a sprawling Irish Catholic family, Lorie began to drink when she was about nine years old and has now just reached twenty-eight—two years off booze. She says she suspects she's a textbook case of genetically inherited alcoholism: "Everyone in my family has had a booze problem; two of my brothers are dead from it, and while my parents are still alive, they're just barely alive. Nothing in my life hasn't been touched—ruined—by alcohol. Two marriages to men I hated. A wild orgiastic stretch in Los Angeles as a 'biker dyke,' which started because the woman who became my first lover marched into the Irish bar I'd gone to one day to get a drink, caught my eye, and said it was time I left that bar and went to a much better bar with her, and I was drunk enough to go with her without bat-ting an eye. Anyway, through some sort of miracle radar, she knew I was gay and was a field ready to be plowed—an expression she used to use a lot. She was into all sorts of s&m whips and leather stuff and, well, that episode lasted a painful year and a half. On about my fourth trip to the emergency room—I don't want to go into the different reasons I had to go there, but let's just say that 'abuse' frequently appeared on my medical charts—and the discovery that my liver was about to give out unless, that instant, I stopped drinking and never took another swig of bour-bon, well . . . let's just say my life changed."

With abstinence abruptly foisted on her, Lorie gained enough clarity quickly enough—helped, she says, by the social worker the L.A. hospital had hooked her up with—to get away from her abu-sive lover and start taking care of herself as if she were human. "I went to some AA meetings held in the hospital and was totally turned off by how schoolmarmish and moralistic they seemed to be. I craved some real advice—about nutrition, for example. I wanted to learn strategies that didn't depend on some kind of re-ligious awakening or moral 'surrender.' In other words, I wanted *help*, not endless lecturing on the state of my sick soul."

Lorie's social worker went down the list of recovery options, and Lorie liked the sound of "Rational Recovery" the best. She also asked for the name of a good book on nutrition, which she'd always been convinced was at the physical root of why she—and everyone else in her family—was so hooked on alcohol. "I didn't have to hear from AA that this was a disease. That wasn't news to me. But I was finally ready to seek treatment for the disease I'd always known I had—well, like I've said, I was scared into it. My choice was stop drinking or die."

Lorie hightailed it to the first Rational Recovery meeting she could find in L.A. and hated it because the man leading it "kept barking at us. Really sort of making us feel stupid because we'd held all these absurd assumptions all our lives that kept us drinking the stuff that was really killing us. Another lecture! Couldn't someone just give me some good nonjudgmental advice? But then other people started talking, and they were funny as all get-out. I know people say this about AA too, but it's the funny stuff I think that really makes the message sink in. Like deciding you're having a health drink when you put grapefruit juice into your vodka. Like assuming getting drunk makes you into a Cleopatra-seductress instead of Phyllis Diller. I don't know—it's a sort of 'you hadda be there' humor. But it was based on recognizing absurdity—the absurdity of holding thoughts and opinions that not only didn't serve you, but were just plain prove-it-on-paper wrong."

The problem for Lorie is that the meeting she'd found was so overwhelmingly heterosexual—and male. "I walked up to one of the women who was there—one of the half dozen, as opposed to twenty-five men—because she seemed like she either might be gay or at least wouldn't be offended if I told her I was gay. As it happens, she wasn't gay, but she was nice and funny and good to talk to and yes, she said, she knew of an openly 'mixed' meeting she'd be glad to take me to sometime. I sort of hooked up with her, got her phone number, all that. Maybe I had my own version of a sponsor in the AA sense, except there was none of that starry-eyed mysterious bolt-from-the-blue spiritual stuff. We were attacking a problem systematically, trading tips about what to do instead of drink."

Lorie says that what she also liked about this non-God approach was its belief that if you had to go to a meeting longer than a year, you should look at what you were doing, because you were doing something wrong. "It was like, there'd be an end to the doctor's visits. I wouldn't have to go for the rest of my life. It's not that there wasn't a maintenance strategy I'd have to employ all my life to keep away from booze, but I didn't have to keep going back to 'class' to employ it. I'd learn stuff I could apply on my own for my whole life, but I wouldn't have to be in 'treatment' for eternity." She found the mixed meeting and met some interesting people there—"some *very* interesting people. Well, who I really mean is Beth, who became my next lover. Beth was this incredibly take-charge lady who ran a health food store, had made it into a big success, and was the answer not only to my romantic dreams, but to my craving for information about nutrition. We quickly became friends, then lovers, and I owe her so much of what I now know about keeping away from alcohol."

Were there no problems?

"Actually," Lorie said. "No. That is, what I was doing to keep from drinking really did keep me from drinking, and it still does. But sure there were problems. I'd attacked my alcoholism like a cow to be slaughtered and dismembered and cut up and sent off to market: it was completely mechanistic. It's true that I sort of left out the feeling part. Even people in Rational Recovery know you've got feelings and that they can knock you sideways when you stop drinking. But their emphasis—which I still think is a good one—is how much those feelings are tied to old, outdated messages you no longer need. That was good to hear, and I could keep laughing about my own absurd adherences to the wrong head trip, but I still had those feelings. They didn't go away because I told them to. I began to get, not so much depressed, as more nervous and edgy. By this time I'd started living with Beth, and I remember one night, after we'd had one more of her perfectly balanced lentil-grain concoctions, just sinking back on the couch and closing my eyes and, almost without realizing I was doing it, I let out this long low moan.

It alarmed Beth: what happened? She instantly thought it was something I ate. I guess I sounded more like I was in pain than I realized. I consulted my stomach: did it hurt? No. Nothing physical hurt, really. But I felt sort of hollow, like there was a wind howling through me that nobody else could hear or feel. Then it occurred to me what the feeling was. Sadness."

Beth, ever the rational-emotive therapist, immediately started asking a series of questions designed to get to the root of the undoubtedly absurd thought processes that resulted in Lorie feeling "sad." But this time Lorie resisted: "Can't you just feel sad sometimes? And not analyze the hell out of it?" She'd quickly moved from sad to mad. "God," she says. "It's like we were living like two little grain-eating p.c. robots!" She tried to explain what was making her angry, but she couldn't find the words. "I'd been so schooled in the rational-emotive therapy model that I kept tripping myself up with qualifications. 'I know this is crazy but' began every halting attempt I made to tell Beth how unhappy I suddenly realized I was.

"Beth understood that it wasn't appropriate to barge in like my therapist, and she suggested we just try to chill out, maybe watch something on TV and just go to bed. That's what we did, but the feeling of anxiety and incompleteness and just plain sadness wouldn't go away. I tossed all night in bed, keeping both of us awake. About six in the morning, Beth groggily reached over and turned on the light. 'Okay, honey,' she said. 'Out with it. You fall out of love with me or something?' I was shocked that this was what she was thinking! And my first response was to do the rote thing—I was about to say 'right thing,' but it had all become rote by now: lead her, step by step, to see the irrational assumption that underlay her assertion, blah blah blah . . ."

Lorie's smile had a slight touch of evil in it. "Then I thought, yeah, that's just what I'll do. Get her at a vulnerable moment where she's sleepily telling me how she feels and get her to analyze the hell out of it! Like she'd tried to do with me the night before, to convince me why I shouldn't feel 'sad.' I didn't have to go far. 'Don't play shrink with me!' she sputtered out at me. And we were silent for a moment. 'You know what I feel like?' I asked her. She said, 'No. What?' 'I feel like we're squirrels in that wheel of a cage, running round and round and round. Couldn't we stop sometimes? Couldn't we just—I don't know, be ourselves? Even if 'ourselves' are a little screwed-up?'"

Beth responded by stretching like a cat and then, also like a cat, curling up under Lorie's arm. 'I feel so tired,' she whispered. 'Soooo tired . . .' 'So do I,' I whispered back. 'Isn't it wonderful?' 'Yeah,' she said, still in a whisper. 'And it's wonderful to feel sad sometimes.' 'And jealous?' 'Yeah. Even jealous.' 'Sort of like being a human being.' 'In a way.' We were lulling ourselves to sleep, two little girls whispering tiny sweet nothings in each other's ears. It felt like the first time in my life that I'd ever truly—in every fiber and molecule of me—relaxed."

Lorie is quick to tell me that when she and Beth woke up later that morning, they did not look into each other's awestruck eyes and acknowledge that they'd had a "spiritual awakening." "We still weren't about to buy all that AA stuff, but what had come back was our sense of humor. And what allowed that to come back was that we'd let up on ourselves. We didn't have to attack every thought and feeling that came out of us, scrutinize it for what Alcoholics Anonymous calls 'stinking thinking'—a phrase, by the way, I have always loathed. It's like our strategies had gotten out of hand; we'd lost sight of the bumbling ambiguous stuff. In a way, we grew to mistrust our feelings and thoughts every bit as automatically and severely as the AA-goers we so much liked to criticize."

Lorie and Beth still adhere to their nutritional regimens and they've started a lesbian and gay Rational Recovery group that's continued to thrive. "But we also have 'silly sessions,'" Lorie says. "Times when we say—shout—sing—dance—whatever the hell we want to. And when we *don't* want to be analyzed but do want to be listened to, we say so. It's like we've moved out of the cage we were in into something that looks more like a playground jungle gym. Play—that's the word. We *play* more. It's as important to keeping me away from Jack Daniels as staying away from refined sugar or reminding myself that I am not, after all, my mother and that Beth is not, after all, my father. And another thing helps a lot too, which is seeing someone as strung out and despairing and hungover as I was walk into one of our meetings, sit down, listen, and start to laugh—for the first time in years."

## The Commonality in Our Clearings

We will always variously "shudder" at (as Lorie did at the thought of Adam's laissez-faire approach to "uncovery") and celebrate the various routes to staying sober we see other people take. But I suppose what Arianne, Adam, Jamie, Grace, Lorie, and Beth all teach me is that, despite their differing approaches to bringing off the feat, staying sober always has roots in self-honesty. Each of them has looked into a kind of special mirror: tried to see and explore and accept and make use of the *reality* they realized they'd been ignoring before—to their peril.

How we react to that reality is our own business and has to do with who we find out we are. There are no "right" or "wrong" ways to come to this self-honesty or to find ways to sustain it, which seems to be at the bedrock of sustaining "sobriety." Self-honesty. Connection—reaching out to, allowing yourself to be reached by, others. Some sort of maintenance. Some sort of down-to-the-soles recognition of self, the kind of recognition Virginia finally came to: that she actually did exist. When you truly start to believe you exist, you start to want to *live*. This, at any rate, seems to be the main commonality I've seen in the lesbians and gay men I've known in recovery.

There's something else magical that happens organically. Perhaps this is already apparent to you, just from entering the lives of the people you've met so far. You stop worrying so much about categories like "gay" or "lesbian" or "straight" or "man" or "woman." Not as some politically correct stance, but because, quite without looking for it, you keep stumbling into other people's *humanness*, which means you keep stumbling into yourself. I believe lesbians and gay men tend to have some fundamentally different gifts and wounds from most heterosexual men and women—gifts and wounds (particularly stemming from that "duplicity expertise" I've gone on about) that we've explored at some length here already. But the "bass drum" that Grace wanted to hear more of in Adam—the hearts that beat in the centers of our duplicitous souls—has a resonance that finally unites us. (Stan can talk to his heterosexual Lutheran farmer-sponsor John *and* wild lesbian Internet-mate vd.) We don't have to do anything about this but listen to the beats of these hearts, listen in the way that Twelve Step meetings often encourage you to listen, without making instant judgments, without feeling the need to contradict or jump in and fix things. Listen with an open mind, heart, and soul—and enjoy it. And, probably, marvel at how listening to other sober people, in and out of "the rooms," somehow makes us feel the strength, for at least one moment longer, to take the next step of whatever path we happen to be on: take it sober.

# 4 The Maze of Sex and Love

Sobriety often seems to me like the bud of a plant very, very slowly opening into a flower—a brilliant big wide flower, like a poppy or a peony. The metaphor works for me on almost every level: the slow revelation of the bud's unsuspected largeness; the growing suppleness and brilliance of the flower's full, varied surfaces; the final daring exposure of its delicate fertile core; its welcoming (but discriminating) receptivity to whatever particular creature or process it needs for regeneration; its movement up and out toward the sun as well as its deepening inward growth; the visible fluttering effect of breezes on the soft petals, so different from the unyielding swing in the wind of the tight little fist of the bud it once was. It is an apt picture of what can happen to a self, a psyche, a soul allowed to "be" what it was meant to be: open, flexible, receptive, and alive.

If the bud finds its full "self" when it becomes a flower, when it interacts with a bee or a bird or the wind or the pollen of another plant, it finds that it is more than itself: it is a "self among other selves." It expands from a lone being to a being giving to and receiving from others. I've offered "connection" as one of the apparently bedrock conditions for recovery maintenance no matter what system of maintenance we employ. But what hasn't been so far made explicit is that connection depends upon one living being *reaching out of itself* toward another: it takes more than passive receptivity; it depends upon an active, open-eyed, and open-hearted search. In other words, we do not seem to attain anything like full self-realization, full consciousness (or full sobriety) by going it completely solo or by refusing to initiate contact with others.

Happily, the desire to initiate that contact does often seem to come as a sort of unlooked-for dividend of sobriety—some alchemical process put into motion simply by staying away from a drink or a drug or whatever "fix" you'd fled to before to eradicate your feelings. Feelings—you can depend on this—*will out* if they're not sledgehammered into the unconscious, and the longer we're able to tolerate our feelings without bolting away from them, the freer we often begin to feel inside. We're not so afraid to reveal who we are; we're not as afraid of other people's judgments of us. In fact, ultimately, we seem simply to fear other people less across the board—in fact, to fear less, period. Remember how Adam said he found himself caring about other people—Jamie, his clients, Grace—in a very surprising (and for him unprecedented) unself-centered way? Lorie and Beth feel most fully "rational" when they're at the recovery group they started and a new lost soul walks in, sits down, and makes contact with them. We do seem to have to reach out of ourselves and join the world to enjoy the world and enjoy being ourselves, maybe simply in order to feel fully *human*, or more pointedly, fully our own eccentric brand of "human."

Again, much of this contact seems to take care of itself. In sobriety/consciousness, you often find yourself treating the guy behind the counter at the dry cleaner's with more good humor, compassion, and consideration than you used to when you'd stumbled in hungover and growling or shuffling with guilt and self-hate. But what about the connections we expect and want to be "intimate," connections we may already be in when we stop drinking or drugging, or may seek to make after we've quit? What about romantic love? What about sex?

Spring breezes suddenly turn into a hot blast from the Sahara. Fresh flowers (in the mind's eye flash-wilted, broken, dead, tromped into dust on the floor by somebody's clomping boot heel) suddenly don't quite provide the adequate metaphor. A new thin voice replaces the violins: ah, Dorothy Parker? Yes (she asks, eternally), "What fresh hell is this?" looking strangely like a fifty-two-year-old Bette Davis stuck forever in film noir black-and-white, forever casting her big hopeless jaded eye on the same old "dump" of a joint.

*Now* we're getting closer.

The bad news you already know is that relationships for all recovering people—gay or straight—often start out being a mess. We may spend so much energy trying to make contact with our own feelings that behaving well or attempting to understand anyone else can seem like advanced quantum physics. So many battle stories, as well as so many hard-won triumphs, emerge here.

Gloria, who even when she was drinking realized that she had nothing in common with her lover Amy (Gloria cared about culture, saw herself as "refined"; she saw Amy as something out of *Ma and Pa Kettle:* "If I'm a Mercedes," Gloria said, "then Amy's an old Chevy pickup truck"), offers one tale that typifies many of our common love-in-recovery dilemmas. At first Gloria thought that the only solution was to leave Amy. "When I was drunk, I could get over the fact that our interests, values, vocabulary—you name it—were irreconcilable. It didn't matter that we had nothing to say to each other. But now, sober, God, it's like I kept looking over the kitchen table and saying to myself: 'Who *is* that woman?' But like a sweet stupid cow, Amy just kept smiling back. You don't have to tell me I sound like an unbearable snob. I know I do. But you wanted to know the truth, and that was the truth. I couldn't stand the woman."

But she also knew, as she said, "It was just too much in early sobriety to change my life that way, leaving her, trying to set myself up alone in a new home. It was all I could do to stay sober. God, I was a cranky two-year-old with her in those first years. I picked on Amy all the time. But I guess I hadn't realized how bad I'd been before then, when I was drunk, and how much Amy had already put up with, how much she'd been willing to put up with."

As months turned into years and Gloria still found herself unwilling to wrench herself away from Amy, and as she got a stronger sense of who she was and what her real values turned out to be, her eyes began to open in a new way to her still-present partner. "It was like I was finally getting to know her for the first time. And although I'd had this mind-set that there was no way our relationship could survive, on a day-to-day basis it *was* surviving. Now, after eleven years of my sobriety, I find something astonishing: I actually care about, even love, Amy! It doesn't matter that she's different from me. She loves me. And I find now that I love her. It's probably the luckiest roll of the dice that I ended up with someone so understanding and forbearing. But she's still with me. She still cares. And she's taught me, by her own patience and persistence, something about what a marriage really means." Gloria pauses for a moment, then admits, "Of course, Amy did go to Al-Anon all that time. I guess I left that part out. But it's an important part. Because I honestly think she would have kicked my butt if she hadn't. I've got about twenty years of being nasty to that poor woman to make up for. But I intend to enjoy every moment of atonement."

Gloria did strike it lucky with Amy; few of the rest of us have or can ever count on having such accommodating partners. You'll find, I hope, a much fuller and more varied view of the experience of "love and romance" in sobriety as we go on here—how we learn to tolerate being vulnerable with each other, cultivate intimacy (sexual and otherwise), and increase our ability to sort out what is workable from what isn't, using our huge variety of experience to provide some sense of not only how we manage to make our own individual peace with "love," but also how our approaches to relationships can actually evolve over time. Just because you don't feel capable of a certain kind of communion right now doesn't mean you can't—or won't—develop a new and larger capacity for intimacy later on.

Various swings of this romantic pendulum will be explored here with any number of resonating effects, but one, I hope, will be to counter some prevailing notions (myths) that gay men and lesbians are two different species. While a lot of gay men are promiscuous and a lot of lesbians do indeed feel "the urge to merge," the opposite is also true of each group, with every imaginable gradation in between connecting us. We simply turn out to be a lot more like each other than unlike each other.

This chapter, perhaps of all the chapters in this book, will be the biggest test of that assertion. It's probably true that most gay men have approached "sex and love" very differently from lesbians. At least, gay men have institutionalized sex (in the form of sex clubs and bathhouses) to a far greater degree than lesbians have, and the disjunction between sex and love—from the allegedly typical lesbian motto "You can't have one without the other" to the allegedly typical gay male "You can't have one with the other"—seems to be dealt with in very different ways by both camps. But once again, sobriety—consciousness—is The Great Softener (all too literally, alas, at its beginning, for a lot of gay men) and The Great Dissolver of Difference. Our barriers become translucent, and when we look through them, we generally see something we can recognize, even if the clothes we're wearing, the words we're saying, and the activities in which we're engaging may appear on the surface to be pretty different.

## Can I Do It Sober?

Dan, at thirty-five, has been sober for nearly five years and he still, as he puts it, "has a hard time—or should I say a soft time—having sex and not getting high. Without poppers, without alcohol to loosen me up, without any of the party drugs I used to take . . . I don't know. I hear that sex can actually be better sober, but I sure haven't experienced it. Not that I don't want to. In fact, my consumption of pornography has just about tripled since I stopped drinking and drugging: I can drum up really hot fantasies. But being with an actual man just still somehow scares the pants off me—whoops. Scares me into keeping my pants *on.*"

This doesn't mean Dan doesn't keep trying. "I've worked the personal ads and actually met some fairly nice guys. But nothing ever catches fire, and it always seems to be my fault. It also didn't help that I entered sobriety in a relationship I'd been in for about four years, which became sexless almost the day after I stopped drinking. Pete just didn't seem to find me attractive anymore. It's like, when I wasn't high, I wasn't wild and sexy and uninhibited. Then I found his membership card to a gay bathhouse and asked him about it. He finally admitted that he liked anonymous sex. He'd been having it even before he and I stopped having sex, and by now, it was the only kind he could get off on. He just couldn't 'objectify' me anymore, he said.

"It made me feel like a totally unattractive worm. I was just crushed. We broke up about six months into my sobriety, and my track record ever since has been pretty abysmal. Then came this guy George, whom I met through the last personal ad I answered. He seemed to promise a totally different experience. He described who he was looking for, and I fit the bill: blond, WASP, slim, 'submissive' in bed. I met him and it turned out I was his type. He obviously found me as attractive as I hoped he would. His eyes lit up when I walked into the room. He was 'technically' my type—

Italian, dark, hairy, stocky. But when he made it clear he wanted to have sex, I freaked.

"I wasn't used to being thought of as attractive—that, anyway, is what I figured out later. All I could concentrate on was what I didn't like about him. My God, it was like I was searching for stuff not to like: the old Joni Mitchell records he played, the awful artwork he had on his walls, his slight New Jersey accent. I played this ice queen with him, which was exactly the opposite of what I thought I wanted to be. I mean, when I answered the ad, I wanted to throw myself into somebody's arms. But now I'd recreated—in the space of two or three dates—the same standoff I'd had way back with Pete. Even stranger, this just seemed to hook George more. We knew nothing about each other really, but we'd managed to get locked into this strange, sexless, miserable war we didn't seem to want to end—all in the space of two or three weeks!"

Turning this war into an arena for communication is something Dan has decided he wants to do. "I don't know if we'll ever become lovers," Dan says, "but I just got so depressed one night after seeing George—and once again repelling his advances, with him looking at me like a puppy who'd just been swatted—that I decided I wanted to break through whatever rut we had so instantly fallen into." Dan also hasn't mentioned anything about being in recovery, partly because George likes to drink beer and he doesn't want to scare George away, even though he's not sure he wants George to stay, either. "I don't know. Maybe I'm still ashamed to admit I'm an alcoholic. And I don't want to get on George's back *again* about something he's 'doing wrong'—drinking beer in front of me, which really does make me uncomfortable. But somehow it's got to be brought up."

Dan's method of sustaining sobriety includes AA, and he has a gay friend Tom whom he says he uses as a sponsor because they're both "in program" and Dan feels comfortable talking to him about most stuff. "Tom told me something that opened my eyes," Dan says. "'You know, you don't have to be madly in love to communicate from the heart,' Tom told him. 'You can do it with the man at the dry cleaner's. You do it with me all the time.' This made me realize that opening up to George, or to anyone else, is something I can pursue no matter what state of connection I'm in with whoever it is. Maybe something in me is lightening up a little, releasing."

Lightening up, releasing, daring, letting go—so much of the language of recovery, or the language of what reassures us, gives us some sense that we might after all be able to take a deep breath and be as fallible and foolish as we fear we are (think of Lorie and Beth shouting silly things to each other in bed). Dan is realizing that the key to whatever lock has made him sexually and romantically unresponsive isn't in George's or anyone else's possession. This is an unnerving realization—that we have to find our own way to any kind of liberation, just as we have to find our way to any kind of recovery—and it's one we seem to ram into whenever we get into each other's beds or lives.

We need to feel connected when we recover, but we can and often do feel this connection only in a meeting or therapeutic context, at least at the beginning. In fact, AA's suggestion that we not enter into a new relationship in the first year of sobriety reflects a lot of our experience that we'd better *not* attempt to connect romantically before we've got a strong and sober enough self to bring into a relationship. Allowing another person "in" romantically or sexually means having to deal with somebody else's differences. We can barely tolerate our own inconsistencies; being saddled with somebody else's can really threaten to put us under (not to mention make us want to escape through the old hatches of booze and drugs). It takes more than initial consciousness of "difference" to break through what can quickly become the hell of a Dan-and-Pete standoff. To use the knowledge of difference you find as you bump into your partner is a yet more refined skill, but sometimes we end up better at it than we think we will.

Cris and Maddy illustrate this vividly: their experience, strength, and hope constitute some of the most powerful examples I've come across that we might actually after all be able not only to love each other, but even to *live* with each other—sober.

## Tolerating Truth, Creating Magic—Sober

Maddy comes from a huge French Canadian farm family; Cris, who is black, comes from an equally huge clan on the outskirts of Atlanta. "I don't know how many people have 'normal' childhoods," Cris laughs, "but I sure don't know what one is. Maddy's pretty weird too, which is probably why we ended up with each other." One thing that unites them is the noise they each had to deal with while growing up—noise and poverty and pretty much random sexual exploration among hordes of brothers and sisters, exploration that amounted in Cris's case to molestation. "Privacy just didn't exist for me," Cris says. "I slept in the same bed with two sisters and a brother until I was thirteen. My brother was three years older. He used to wrestle around with us every night for a couple hours before he finally fell asleep. My two younger sisters used to hold on to me to get away from his grabbing. I'd poke him with my elbows and knees, fight with him as hard as he wanted to fight. I think I knew very early on that it was sexual for him. Then it became obvious. He started calling us his 'harem.' He'd jump on us and try to rub his penis against whoever he could get to lie still. He was also almost always drunk—God knows where he got the stuff, but he smelled like cheap wine from the time he was twelve years old. He'd just get rougher when he was drunk. It made me furious, his grabbing at me and my sisters, which just seemed to turn him on more. I can't believe our parents didn't know what was going on; they were in the next room, with two babies in cribs sleeping with them. Hell, I remember shouting really outrageous stuff that Mama and Daddy must have heard: 'Get your damned dick away from me!' But they just ignored us. All I remember about my mama and daddy is that they were exhausted. Daddy worked two shit jobs; Mama was a nurse's aide in the hospital. They just kept working and having babies and letting their family see to itself. If anyone was the mother and father, it was me. At least, I was the only one who showed any kindness to my little sisters. My brother sure as hell didn't."

Cris's hatred of her brother was only partly why she left home right after graduating high school: "I knew I was gay, I think, by the time I could walk and talk. Anyway, I knew I was different. I hated all the little-girl shit kids in school were into. I guess I always felt tougher than everybody else. I was always getting into fights. I kept my hair cut short. Maybe it was also because I felt I had to protect my little sisters from my damned brother all the time. It was like I was in some kind of war with him, and I wasn't gonna let him win. Anyway, I started sneaking into Atlanta and hanging out at gay bars, drinking my head off when I was still a teenager. Sometimes I wouldn't come home for days at a time. My parents didn't seem to give a shit. I got involved with all kinds of drunken women, especially lipstick lesbians. God, I love a beautiful woman! I've never understood why so many lesbian activists wanna dress like lumberjacks, even though I guess I've done my share of combat boots and flannel shirts. But hell, the thing I love about women is that they're *women*. I guess I'm as attracted to a beautiful, made-up, classy, sexy lady as any straight man is. Anyway, I had my share. And while I somehow got through high school and did okay—one teacher tried to get me a scholarship to the University of Georgia, although I didn't have the least interest in college—I couldn't wait to get away, travel around the country, check out New York and Boston and Chicago and San Francisco, which is what I did. When I think of it now, I became as big a womanizer as I knew my brother wanted to be. Maybe I was just in competition with him; I don't know. I hated him, but I also envied that he was a man—older, stronger, getting pretty much any woman he wanted."

Cris's "womanizing" was fueled by her drinking and, later, drug taking: "Dammit, when I think of how many thousands of dollars I've spent on getting high. I'd be rich now if I had even one-quarter of what I spent on drugs and booze." When the drugs became heroin, Cris nearly died: "I was so used to drinking six times as much as anybody else, I thought I could do the same thing with smack. But I nearly killed myself with an overdose. Ended up in a San Francisco state hospital. They put me in a rehab, which connected me with AA and NA and all of the other 'A's.' I guess I was ready to stop. I was exhausted. I'd had enough. So I got sober."

At a lesbian and gay AA meeting in San Francisco, she met Maddy. "God," Cris says, remembering when she first saw Maddy, "she was this—*flighty* little thing. Like some little spirit out of the forest. Tiny, slim, sweet, pale—almost like she wasn't real." Maddy was equally attracted to Cris. "It helped that we both came from big families," Maddy says. "I guess I knew right off that Cris understood what it meant to fight for attention—for love, for space, for friends. In my house, for *food*." Maddy had as many brothers as Cris had sisters. "Sometimes I think we're like photographic negatives of each other," Maddy says. "Cris with one older brother and all those sisters; me with one older sister and an army of brothers. And of course, me being white, Cris being black. From the start it was like we fit each other, even if our experiences growing up, apart from the big families, were pretty different. My mom and dad were fierce Catholics. I got a big dose of guilt along with my mother's milk. They had all these kids, you'd think they wouldn't have been so uptight over sex, but they were. We weren't allowed to go even to PG movies—and damn, the whipping you'd get if you so much as whispered a four-letter word. But I know Cris sort of became the 'man' of her house. I survived in a different way. I was the quiet little wallflower, trying to erase myself, almost, so that I wouldn't get into trouble. My dad took his belt off and used it on whatever kid's bottom was nearest at the least provocation. I was terrified of getting beat up by him, the way my brothers always did."

Maddy says she escaped into a private dreamworld: "I'd invent perfect playmates for myself while I was doing farm chores. I see now they were all versions of my older sister. She was different from everybody else in the family. She did really well in school. She ended up going to a Catholic college when I was twelve; she'd skipped a couple grades and got out of the house at sixteen. I envied her so much! She'd gotten away! I so longed to get away too."

Like Arianne, Maddy felt drawn to witchcraft as a kind of spiritual, female-affirming escape. "That's about when my interest in witchcraft started. If only there were some spell I could cast, something that would make my sister come for me and take me away." Maddy's interest in witches and magic was something she knew, given her devout Catholic family, she had to keep secret. "I'd save up money and send away for books and pamphlets on pagan rituals and earth religions centered on goddesses, and ask that they be mailed in plain brown wrappers, like pornography or something. I actually called a bookstore in New York that I'd read in one magazine was run by women who were openly witches— dropped about a dozen quarters into a pay phone to do it—and asked them to recommend titles. In high school, I had one friend—a girl as quiet as me but who was secretly a lot more adventurous. She used to steal pot from her older brother and she'd roll it into joints and we'd get stoned after school. I'd tell her about the incantations I was learning about. We'd try to cast spells on people we didn't like. I just sort of got lost back then—lost in my dreams, lost in the pot, lost in all those spells. . . ."

Maddy's version of witchcraft had turned into a more general New Age spirituality by the time she met Cris. "Partly what got me off the witchcraft thing was discovering how many lesbians were attracted to that whole 'goddess' movement. It scared me. I realize now that I longed to explore my sexuality, but I just couldn't imagine ever having the guts to try. So I followed my older sister's example and went to the same Catholic college she went to. Maybe if I just became a good Catholic again, things would work out." Maddy laughs. "The college was in San Francisco, the gay mecca of the universe! I was so scared of everybody. That's when the pot got out of hand. That's when I started to get really paranoid—to the point, once, of getting locked up in a mental hospital, after I'd tried to kill myself. I was in my last year of college. I was so lonely. I sort of knew I liked women, but I didn't have the guts to act on it. I climbed up to the roof of my dorm, which was only about three stories high, but high enough. I had smoked three joints of very powerful stuff. I was determined to throw myself off. Nothing seemed possible anymore. I couldn't imagine a place for me in the world. But I turned out not to be very good at self-annihilation. I did jump. I can still remember the terror but also the exhilaration of that moment when I threw myself off. However—story of my life!—I landed in a bush, which broke my fall and nearly broke my leg. I ended up with a sprained ankle, whimpering, whimpering. Oh God, I was such a mess. A college custodian found me and called an ambulance. I was so incoherent, they didn't know what to do with me, but they did know I'd just jumped off the roof. So

I got locked up for a while. Don't remember much about it, except they suggested that I stop smoking pot. That pot was what had sent me over the edge."

Maddy, too, decided that pot was the problem, which eventually brought her to the same Twelve Step rooms Cris was then haunting. "Talk about love at first sight: it was incredible," Cris said. "I just saw this lost, lovely little girl in the corner and that was it. She was mine. I knew she just had to be mine." Maddy was (as always) ready to be "saved." "It's like Cris solved all my problems at once. I was too terrified to walk up to anyone, much less any woman I thought might be gay. Cris just steamrolled in and took over. It was amazing, back then, that first time. She took me back to her apartment and very simply began to kiss me, make love to me. I'd never been hugged much before, much less caressed like Cris caressed me. It was—incredible."

But now, two years later, in the same apartment, sleeping in the same bed Cris first took her to that magical first night, Maddy is baffled by the change that has come over both of them. "In a word," Maddy said, "it's depression. I feel like I've finally gotten everything I could possibly want in a relationship—that perfect girlfriend I used to dream about back in Canada as a little kid—and slowly, day by day, it feels like something has just drained out of me. It just makes Cris angry, me slowly shutting down like this. It's not that we've stopped having sex; we still make love. But I guess I just don't feel *there* most of the time. Cris comes home from her job; I come home from mine. She's apprenticing at a stained-glass studio and working as a waitress in a lesbian and gay coffee shop. I've got some stupid clerical job at a law firm. Maybe that's a part of the problem: Cris always seems to be doing what she wants to do. I always seem to be doing what I'm handed. I don't know. The only solution I can think of is to get high again. At least on pot I had more access—more access to my dreams. To what I could be. Now, 'clean,' I just feel blank. Scared. Incapable. NA meetings simply haven't been enough to make me feel less blank and scared and incapable. I came across my old drug dealer's number the other day and nearly dialed it. Then I remembered I'd heard she'd gone into rehab. God, I thought, can't even count on a drug dealer to stay high anymore."

"She pisses me off," Cris says. "Damn, it's one thing to be quiet and dreamy. It's another thing to sit there like a slug. I mean, it's typical that she'd be thinking of going back to pot. Great solution, honey! Fuck yourself up some more. Leave the world even more than you already do. Sometimes I just want to *shake* Maddy awake. Where does she go in that head of hers? It's like she takes these long vacations away from me, even when we're in the same room. I'll be railing away about my day, about the asshole straight guy who came because he's obviously turned on by lesbians, and how I cursed him out. Anyway, Maddy'll be there, looking sad and quiet, a million miles away. It's like she already *is* stoned, like she has gone back to smoking pot. It's making me feel—God, I don't like admitting it. But it's making me feel more than angry. It's like I'm getting sadistic. It's like I want to *hurt* her—hit her, slap her, kick her, make her *feel* something. It's making me feel like I want to drink again! God, two lesbians in recovery and all we're doing is making each other want to get high."

Maddy has always been aware of a violent undercurrent in Cris; it's partly what's made her shut down, she says: "It's like my dad all over again. Me hiding in the corner hoping he won't notice me so I won't get hit. Sometimes, I'm really afraid that Cris will haul off one day, and . . ." She shudders and looks out the window. "I don't know how to change, how to please her. It's like there's something dead inside of me. Even Cris can't reach this part of me; wake it up."

However, Cris and Maddy—in the wake of couple's therapy

sessions, which they've recently embarked upon—aren't entirely unable to "see" or "hear" each other. They've begun to see, anyway, how intricately and unconsciously they play into each other's secret fearful expectations. Oddly, what Cris has discovered is that not only is she angry at Maddy's internal disappearing act, but she is also jealous of her ability to "vanish." "I'm starting to see that I was exhausted as a kid, more exhausted than I knew," Cris says now. "Maddy became like my frightened little sisters—somebody I had to take care of, protect, caress, make feel better. Drinking allowed me to vanish. I never liked pot, made me too spacey. Too unable to fight. But wine, beer, scotch—man, it brought out the tigress in me. I was in such a war with my brother—it's like I never had any choice but to fight. Maybe some part of me was jealous of my sisters. It's like *they* were all stoned little Maddys. I wish I'd had somebody like me to take care of me! I never thought of it until we started talking to a therapist, but there might be a frightened, sweet little girl underneath all this kick-ass exterior. Maybe it's as simple as what I just said: I want someone to take care of me for a change."

Maddy has discovered some surprises too, specifically that what feels "dead" in her is any ability to feel and express anger and rage. Maddy had always been clear about some yin/yang aspects of her attraction to Cris—that Cris would "take over" her life, her body, her feelings in a way Maddy herself never could, in a way not even pot allowed her to feel "taken over." But she'd never quite seen the connection to her own anger. Until one day when, to the surprise of both, it came roaring out of her—"luckily," she says, "in our therapist's office. I don't know what would have happened if we didn't have her to intervene." Cris was needling Maddy about a familiar subject. Cris explained that she'd just come from a "dump" session with her sponsor Marsha in which, as it turned out, she *hadn't* dumped her anger at the perversely passive Maddy as she thought she had; she'd merely stoked the coals and intensified the flames.

Once in their therapist's office, she glared at Maddy: "You hate your job, but you never even talk about looking for another. And you resent the hell out of me for doing what I want to do. Why are you wasting your time at that damned place? They're never going to promote you, especially with you hiding yourself in a corner all the time like a little mouse. It pisses me off that you don't even think about being ambitious."

Maddy's expression was impassive while Cris went on, until the last sentence. "Never even think about being ambitious?" Maddy said. "How do you know what I'm thinking about?" There was a new note of tension in her voice, as close as Maddy generally got to anger.

Cris fought her first urge, which was to launch into yet another attack about how Maddy never talked about her feelings, never talked about anything inside her. She tried to remember the approach that her sponsor had, just two hours before, encouraged her to take with Maddy: not to be defensive, but to *hear* what Maddy was saying, the way she was able to listen even to provocative or upsetting stuff in AA or NA meetings and not hit the roof. So she took a deep breath and segued:

"You're right that I don't know what you're thinking about. It's always seemed to me you're afraid to let me know." Cris might have been calming one of her younger sisters; her voice was soothing. Gently, she asked: "What are you afraid of, Maddy? Let me know."

Maddy closed her eyes for a moment. "You know the only thing that comes into my mind? That time I threw myself off the roof of my dorm. I never told you something about that."

Cris looked at her expectantly, her eyes asking Maddy to go on.

"I *loved* throwing myself off that roof."

"Did you want to die?"

"No," Maddy said. "I wanted to fly. And for a moment, the moment I took that leap, it almost felt like I could."

## How to Fly without Dying

"I can understand that, wanting to fly. I've always wanted to fly. It's probably why I got high so much. Something about the very word 'high'—it was like we could just float over everything else. Is that what you mean?"

"You're always putting words in my mouth," Maddy said, her tone tense again. "You always act like you know what I'm thinking." Maddy was silent for a second. "You don't have the first fucking clue what I'm thinking."

The words hit Cris like a slap. She had literally never heard Maddy use the word *fucking* before. And she'd never heard Maddy use this tone, which had gone beyond tense to quietly rageful. Maddy was *mad*. But Cris willed herself not to attack back, not at all easy for her. She took a deep breath, and she went back into what she thinks of as "sponsor mode" ("When I'm about to blow, I always think to myself, now what would Marsha say?"): "Where's the hurt, Maddy? What hurts right now?"

"Oh, don't pull that caring shit on me," Maddy said. "I've been sitting here like an open wound for two years in front of you, and you haven't even noticed. Not really. You're just always mad at me. Don't pretend like you care what *hurts*. You wanna know what hurts? *You* hurt. You hurt me every time you tell me I'm nothing, that my job is nothing, that I don't have any dreams. I have a lot of dreams." Maddy's voice was trembling, somewhere between rage and tears. The tears finally won out, and she started to cry.

Cris said: "I'm sorry I piss you off. But I do care. Go with me a little on this. Tell me what's coming up for you now. I want to

hear it." Cris tried to think of what might be a good next "therapeutic" question. How could she help Maddy make connections
to other times in her life when she'd felt the same way? She almost asked, "What does this remind you of in your childhood?"
But she stopped herself; she knew suddenly that if she'd taken
that frontal approach, Maddy would have resisted—in the mood
she was in, she might have thrown something at Cris for trying to
play "shrink" so baldly. Anyway, Maddy didn't need prodding
now, and Cris was sensitive enough to know this, to know that all
she had to do (for once) was get out of Maddy's way. Maddy was
ready to make her own connections. At first, it was as if she were
talking to herself; then she managed to focus on the therapist,
and finally on Cris. Her words gained force as she was slowly able
to face Cris, talk to her directly about what she'd held back for
what seemed like a lifetime:

"I have gone through my whole fucking life trying to pretend
I didn't exist, trying not to impose, trying not to get in anybody's
way. I'm sick of trying to disappear. I'm sick of everyone looking
at me like I was some pathetic little orphan. Sometimes—sometimes I hate you, Cris. Sometimes I wish you'd just *shut up*. Do
you know how much you go on about every little damned detail
of your day? Sometimes I can't believe your gall—your fucking
*presumptuousness* in thinking that anyone cares about every last
little breath you take. What makes you think you've got the right
to monopolize everybody's attention all the time? Don't you
know other people exist in the world?"

Maddy was all but yelling now and talking directly to Cris.
Then she stopped. It was as if she'd somehow flitted out of herself,
seen this strange rageful woman—and it shocked her. Her voice
quieted. "I'm sorry," she said. "I don't mean it. God, when I flare
up like that, it scares me. I suddenly realize why I loved to smoke
pot—it kept me from exploding like this. But, well, maybe I do

need to say how angry I am. I don't want to have to apologize for it all the time. Angry—and jealous. I thought I had to be a witch to get my way, to cast strange spells on people to get them to notice me, love me, give me what I wanted. You just went out there and took what you wanted. You've always known how to fly. I never knew, except by getting high. But I'm so very, very angry that I'm still here on the ground. And I'm so angry that I don't have pot to help me forget that I'm stuck down here. I just don't know how to get out of this awful trapped feeling. It's how I always felt as a little girl. All those damned boys around me—all my brothers. Wrestling and shouting and getting into trouble and getting whipped by my dad. It was like they were from some other planet than I was.

"You know, we had a lot of cats on the farm; they kept the mice in line. But there was this one—we used to call her 'L'il Noogie'; she was the only one of a particular litter to survive. Her mother had some strange blood disease that she passed on to her kittens, and they all died but this one, L'il Noogie. I don't know; maybe the mother freaked or something, but she wouldn't let L'il Noogie nurse. So my mother let me take care of the kitten. I fed it from a bottle. Loudest little kitten you ever heard—can't believe the noise that little creature could make, meowing! Anyway, she was always looking for a nipple. She used to climb up on my head, searching through my hair for her mother's nipple. It was like my hair was her mama! Then one day a tomcat, this real kick-ass tom who was the farm's champion mouser, he gets L'il Noogie's attention. The kitten was like, I don't know, fascinated by that tomcat, as if she couldn't believe any cat could be so confident. And there was nothing that tomcat wouldn't do— leap across the room without ever touching the floor, climb any tree, dangle off the top of the barn—he was fearless. L'il Noogie just looked at him wide-eyed and tried to follow him. Somehow she pulled herself up the barn and got on the roof one day because the tomcat was up there. She crept real close to the edge of the highest overhanging eave and watched him make a flying leap to a maple tree. Nutty kitten thought she could do it too."

Maddy started to cry again, this time more quietly. "She broke her neck. But I like to think she knew, for that one last moment of her life, what it was like to fly."

That this was a moment of transformation—not just a moment of increasing Cris's "knowledge" of Maddy—only became clear the next day, after their couple's session. At breakfast, Maddy announced a decision she said she'd come to. "I'm quitting my damned job," she said. "I'm gonna take some time off. Maybe I'll even take a little trip by myself." She looked a little warily at Cris, as if expecting to be told that she was out of her mind. But Cris, hearing the force in Maddy's voice, which was full of a new conviction, just beamed at her. "That sounds real good, honey," she finally said. "Real good. About time you started doing what you wanted."

You can fly without dying—*or* getting high: this is what Cris wanted to say to Maddy and didn't have to. Maddy began to see that there were risks she could manageably take, that she could after all make an attempt to take a stand, try to get something she wanted, live from her heart. It transformed her view of "sobriety": being sober didn't mean you didn't take chances. In fact, it required you to take "chances," to take actions toward a clearer, better, freer, happier, more responsible and responsive life. But this realization—the transformative moment for Maddy (which transformed Cris's view of Maddy as well)—came first from acknowledging at least a tiny portion of the anger Maddy had never before been able to address, much less express.

Maddy and Cris have since come to explore, both in and out of therapy and Twelve Step rooms, that they really *are* in many ways mirror images of each other's fears and dreams: each has explored a realm of self the other felt was blocked off. But it's not enough, as they now know, simply to see a "lost part of self" acted out by someone else. We need to find and express our own lost parts and regain the capacity to give them life. There's something magical and inexplicable about how we learn to do this. Cris did all she could for Maddy when she simply quieted and let Maddy speak, when she ceased speaking *for* Maddy. This didn't guarantee that Maddy would come to a breakthrough. It just gave her space to be herself without censure or judgment or "translation." Cris is clear that this ability to listen openly, without clamping down on what you heard with all defenses firing, is a product of spending so many years listening in AA, listening without feeling that you were being called on to agree or disagree, advise, or even comment. You could let other people say and think what they had to say and think. You didn't constantly have to "translate," either to yourself or to whomever you decided in that instant "desperately" needed your advice or input. *Translate* has become Maddy's catchword now, when Cris starts to monopolize the airwaves and "analyze" what Maddy is "really" thinking. "Stop translating," Maddy now says. "I don't need a translator." And then she makes a stab at saying what she thinks and feels herself.

## Embracing (Not Just Tolerating) Differences

I've given so much space to Maddy and Cris's story because the moment of "transformation" that their story embodies is so difficult to capture: I only know how to convey it by attempting to relate something of the complex texture of (in this case) Cris's and Maddy's lives and their styles of communication, which takes time to spin out. Most of us quickly learn that there's no way that a reductive list of "what to say" and "what not to say" could ever capture the elusive magic that we finally learn can connect us, help us to grow—and transform us. The connection to how many of us learn to listen nondefensively in Twelve Step rooms seems especially apt to me: so many of us have enjoyed that similar humbling experience that the world is not dying for us to advise it, that in fact it takes *time* to understand someone and to sort out other people's assumptions from our own. This sorting out is especially crucial and difficult in our love relationships because the more intimate we are with other people, the more we blindly, reflexively project old family dramas and assumptions onto other people. We end up not seeing who we're actually with: unconsciously, we've turned them into stand-ins for Mom, Dad, our older or younger brothers or sisters, our first lovers, our junior high gym teachers, and so on. (Our next story will attempt to nail that pervasive problem in the heart.)

But it's right to wonder—and normal to worry about—what happens next, now that Maddy and Cris have learned to "hear" each other and even begin to take actions that promise to move them into freer, happier territory. What happens after Maddy quits her job, maybe takes a trip by herself? Is her life "solved" now? Has she forever banished her fears? Has she now captured all those lost parts of self she had psychically rejected? Have all the blocks in her relationship with Cris been eradicated? In a word, is she—and is Cris—"cured"?

Transformation opens a door to an awakening—and this may be the greatest lesson of sobriety for many of us—but the real work happens once we've walked through that door. Just as there seems to be no such thing as a cure for alcoholism or drug addiction, there is no cure for the reflexive fears and assumptions that continually pop up, like ogres in a medieval allegory, and stop us cold. These fears and assumptions are unconscious; they are part of our habitual response to the world. "Feelings are not facts" runs one AA slogan—a way of reminding us that feelings do not constitute the whole of our current in-the-moment reality; they are often tied to our earliest resentments, cravings, jealousies, and rages. They are a kind of instant paint that colors the person, thing, or situation we're confronting in old, familiar, but often completely false ways. Feelings are, however, powerful and they're packed with information about how we habitually see and react to the world. So much of the self-reflection called for in the Twelve Steps is geared to helping us *see* the "habit" or reflex in our feelings so that we can begin to separate ourselves from it enough to behave in a way that will serve us better. The central lesson of recovery might simply be said to be this: you can have a feeling and not act on it. You can have a feeling and act against it. This is radical news to every alcoholic and addict I've ever met. And in the arena of love relationships, it's a continuing revelation—we seem to need to learn it again and again. We need to cultivate moments of awareness as assiduously as Maddy's farmer dad cultivated his crops: expand them, *live* them throughout each day.

We're also wise to expect that we'll stumble and regress on a very regular basis. Maddy is no doubt destined to experience some of her own fearful darkness again; Cris will no doubt once more "hog the airwaves" in her attempts to fix and protect the Maddys of the world. But both women now know some other ways of communicating with each other; they now know what it feels like at least to touch rejected aspects of self, bring them into the light, and try them on at least briefly for size. Cris says, "You know what Step in the Twelve Steps has been helping me the most? The Tenth Step. 'Continued to take personal inventory and when we were wrong promptly admitted it.' I used to think this was superfluous—like, okay, we already had the Fourth Step. Why is a whole Step devoted to reminding us to keep doing the Fourth Step? Now I see—especially when Maddy starts to drive me up the wall—why it's so important. A whole Step is devoted to telling us to *keep doing the work of staying conscious*, keep pulling on the sails to change course if the boat starts veering off course. *Stay present.*"

So much of what might be called growing up in sobriety—growing beyond the "No, I won't do it!" stage of a two-year-old—means learning to take a new look at our assumptions about love, to "stay present" for the revelation that they *are* assumptions and not necessarily God-given unassailable truths. (The AA slogan "Feelings are not facts" gives us a clue about a similar relativity: that our "feelings" are often the product of defensive assumptions rather than an indication of some objective reality.) This doesn't mean we can change their essential character; in fact, that's probably a doomed pursuit. But we might be able to explore how to adapt to the urgencies of that character, find ways up here in the "real world" of getting what our cravings for love want us to get—again, to *behave* in a way that our full conscious minds now tell us will serve us better. This is exactly what we seek in recovery from drugs or alcohol, after all: not only to honor or at least acknowledge our motives, but to find ways of satisfying those motives that won't kill us.

Maddy will always in some way feel like that suicidal little kitten, L'il Noogie, but in confronting the fears that have created this internal icon of pathos, she has begun to find the tomcat in her, as well. She will always seek comfort and guidance—the kitten part of her will always be needy—but she now sees that her range of feelings and options isn't *limited* to being that kitten. Unconsciously, the love fantasy she yearns for—the protective, adventurous, sexual extrovert that Cris so readily represents for her—has nudged her to confront these fears the more she's become conscious of it. She now sees that she not only wants someone like Cris, but wants to *be* more like Cris herself. Her repertoire of possibilities—her very self-view—has widened. She's a larger person than she was before.

These revelations would have been impossible had Maddy and Cris been drinking and drugging throughout this episode. Sobriety clears the way for revelations of all kinds, whether we label them "negative" or "positive." If you're drunk or high, you cannot do the kind of searching, fearless moral inventory that AA's Fourth Step asks you to do for a simple reason: drunk or high, you can't see the full territory. You can only see reality—and the partner you may be involved with—through a very tiny pinhole. Any "inventory" you may seek to take in this state is doomed to be woefully incomplete.

## Seeing Who's Really There

Dmitri and Mark are two men in their early thirties who are also discovering that becoming larger as human beings can happen only if they remain sober for sobriety's own sake—not, as they had once thought, solely to keep their relationship together, but, more primally, each for his own sake. "You have to make a commitment to be conscious *yourself* before you can make any kind of profitable investigation of who you really are, or who anyone else is," Dmitri says.

How Dmitri and Mark got to this sense of sober "largeness" was certainly fueled for each of them by a fairly strict adherence to their AA and NA sponsors' and shared therapist's suggestions, even if they ignored one of those suggestions right from the start—not to get into a relationship in their first year. Dmitri says, "We seemed to have the simultaneous revelation that we needed to stop drinking and using, and this bonded us, right in the therapy group where we met."

However, navigating their relationship in early sobriety—after each made a pact to get sober, they fell in love almost immediately—has required more than just increasing sober "consciousness." They've had to change some behaviors too. The lessons they've learned in recovery have nudged them into a more continual Tenth Step wake-up or reality-check process that tells them how much they're projecting out of habit and old fears and how much they're actually responding to who's in front of them at the moment. The idea that they might be able to *embrace* their differences, not just tolerate them, has turned out to be most helpful.

"I'd been involved with a series of lovers," Dmitri says, "from college on, none of whom lasted for longer than three years, before I met Mark. I always seemed to get to the same point, the same kind of standoff. Basically, it always ended in intolerable bickering, made worse by endless drinking. I turn into a nasty drunk, the way my father was when he drank. I don't think my dad's an alcoholic like I became—I mean, he gets nasty when he drinks, but that's pretty much only at parties. He doesn't drink nonstop at home, the way I eventually did. It was always embarrassing to my family that I got so obnoxious: I'm from a Greek family, and Greeks aren't supposed to be drunks! I got sober partly by going to AA, but mostly in therapy, both group and one-and-one. My family doesn't know anything about that rite of passage. I told them I went to some allergist who said I was allergic to alcohol and shouldn't drink it. Actually the therapist I go to is an alcoholism counselor who's turned into my regular therapist. He's got a group—not AA, just regular group therapy—which has helped to keep me sober. But I go to AA too. Frankly, right now I need all the help I can get.

"Sometimes I get really depressed when I realize how powerful my urge is to nitpick whoever I fall in love with—I just feel, sometimes, like I'll always be trapped in that mode I obviously learned in childhood. My parents were born in a small town in Greece, and, Jesus, if Mark has learned anything from getting involved with me, it's how passionately self-absorbed Greek families can be. You know, most Greeks don't leave home until they get married—which means if they don't get married by thirty-five, they're still living with Mommy and Daddy and still basically acting like six-year-olds. And the bond between a Greek father and son—*whoeee!* I don't know how to begin to tell you how strong and ambivalent *that* little love affair is. My dad came over here at seventeen, knowing no English, and by twenty-five he'd set up a thriving car dealership, which made him enough money to go back on a triumphant trip to his hometown, complete with a fancy new Buick that he had shipped over and drove down the main street to the house of the 'best family,' in the hope of wooing one of that best family's daughters. There were three of them, and my dad—negotiating it like a business deal with the girls' father—settled on the middle one. She was eighteen, and within a month of getting married, she was on a ship bound for New York with a husband she barely knew. In other words, she just got handed from father to husband, dumped in a strange land with strange customs and language, and forced to fend for herself. They lived first in Brooklyn. My mother still talks about trying to figure out how to be 'American,' which in those days, in Brooklyn, meant wearing poodle skirts, going to the grocery store with your hair up in curlers, and chewing gum. She felt totally at sea, but she soaked up every little detail, learning English in record time, and as my father's business got more successful, realized that there were 'classier' ways to be American than the lower-middle-class model shoved into her face in Brooklyn. They moved out to the north shore of Long Island into a nice new suburban house, and they had kids—me and my younger sister. But my mother never quite gave up her resentment at being yanked out of her father's home and made to live with this strange man. My parents fought constantly. My sister and I were always refereeing, always trying to get them to stop yelling at each other. Of course the flip side of this—how we had to be in public—was exactly opposite. You've never seen a prettier, better dressed, or better behaved family in a restaurant or at church than my family. Appearances meant everything: you were only as good as the image you portrayed out in the world. So I learned two modes early on: fight like maniacs at home, and act like you're perfect when you walk out the door. It's like they trained me to be a raging alcoholic: by high school, I was sneaking out to drink with friends after school or late at night on weekends, then dousing myself with mouthwash and forcing myself to 'act straight'—that, ironically, was the phrase we used—when I got home."

Mark's childhood scenario also placed a huge emphasis on conveying the right appearance in public, with some of the same emotional damage. "It's weird—I mean, the stuff my parents wanted me and my two brothers to do and be was stuff they obviously valued but couldn't pull off themselves. Like, my father is this big silent lump of a guy, unathletic and out of shape, but the one thing he wanted us to do was succeed in sports, I guess like he never could. So we were shoved off to baseball, basketball, football, and other sports camps in the summer and told we had to try out for teams in junior and senior high. Basically we learned that to be a 'man' you had to be hot shit at sports. The only thing I liked about those camps, especially from junior high on, were all the hot teenaged guys, even if they didn't have much use for me. I also loved smoking pot and drinking beer, which the older teenagers always seemed to get hold of.

"But, back home, with all his pushing me to get into sports, my father was a damned couch potato. Oh, he'd been on his track team back in high school and had some kind of minor success at the fifty-yard dash, but basically he was an athletic washout. My mother picked up the academic side—it was the same deal, really.

When we came home with anything less than an A on our report cards, we got lectured and had to explain in great detail why we had 'failed.' In fact, my mother wasn't any great shakes at school herself. But it's like she wouldn't tolerate our being anything less than perfect. My two brothers—one's older, one's younger—were okay on the sports side, although I was a total waste at sports. I hated them; I hated the competition and pretty soon began to hate anything physical at all."

Mark's experience of recovery and addiction were insidious: "I loved drinking from the first sip of beer, getting high from the first toke off a joint. They just made me feel . . . *powerful,* I guess. I continued smoking pot and tried mescaline in high school and college, but I didn't like the spacey way hallucinogens made you feel. I got hooked on ecstasy after college and did "Special κ" when I wanted to go out and have sex. They didn't make me feel spacey; they made me feel terrific, and horny."

Mark didn't think these up-to-the-minute "designer" club-goer drugs were "addictive" or made a mess out of you as long as you controlled the amounts you took, "especially," Mark says, "of Special κ. There's something called a κ-hole that friends warned me about, where you'd just suddenly become immobilized, wouldn't be able to move a limb. You'd be paralyzed, really. Then I found out it's the drug they use to sedate animals, including elephants! God, I was playing with my life. Not only because I could have passed out permanently from a deep enough κ-hole, but because I simply didn't care about who fucked me or whether or not it was 'safe.' Amazingly, I still test negative on the HIV test. People wonder, 'Why do young gay men have unsafe sex?' Well, there are probably a million reasons. But get off on 'κ' and you'll find out one of the biggest ones. I scared myself into sobriety. I knew I had to stop, because I almost didn't come to after one descent into that hole, and I really panicked. I went to a clinical psychiatrist who put me on Zoloft—he just assumed I was depressed, which I guess I was—but it was sort of trading one drug for another, even if the replacement was a hell of a lot safer. But I told him I wanted to get off everything, and because he wasn't much help in getting me to do that, I hooked up with the same counselor Dmitri is seeing. That's how Dmitri and I met—in that counselor's group."

That group is where Mark and Dmitri learned about each other's childhoods and about how many similar fears and assumptions they shared, and it's where they fell in love. Now they realize they share another similarity in their reactions to their parents: they are quick—after reciting the usual complaints about their upbringings—to defend their parents as well, in what both now realize are similar ways. "My parents may fight at home all the time," Dmitri says, "but they do love each other and they're as devoted as Dobermans to their kids. As awful as they can sometimes be, I've never not felt loved—more than loved. They live for my sister and me; we're the most important people in their lives." Mark says that his family also demonstrates a fierce cohesiveness and loyalty: "My mom and dad may berate us for not being 'as good as we could be,' but listen to them talk to anyone outside the family and all they give their kids is praise. It's funny, sometimes I'll walk into the living room and hear my mom on the phone and going on about how brilliant somebody is, and then realize she's talking about me. It'd be nice if she told *me* this stuff, but it's nice to know she spouts it off to everybody else." Their families' brands of self-loyalty have rubbed off on Mark and Dmitri in another similar way: "We both have this ideal of one lover—one human being we can build a life with and be monogamous with, have a family," says Dmitri. Mark agrees: "Dmitri is the first gay man I've ever met who seems to have the same relationship ideals that I do. That's still what makes me think we might have a chance, even if we are in our first year of sobriety."

Neither has been able to engineer this kind of devoted monogamous relationship with anyone else, however, although each has been involved with a series of lovers, both starting in college. Dmitri has had the greater success of the two in sustaining his relationships timewise, despite the horrendous effects of drugs and alcohol. He hit the two- or three-year mark with each of his four lovers, but he admits that none of these unions was happy for more than moments, and, regardless of his fiercely held ideal that a "real" love should be monogamous, none of his past relationships was monogamous. "I wish I could say it was always the other guy," Dmitri says, "but sometimes it was me. I'd just get so mad at whoever I was with, and so frustrated, that sometimes I'd connect on the phone line with some guy who fit my sexual fantasy bill, or seemed to."

Sexual fantasy was a big part of the "frustration" Dmitri felt, and still feels. "I've always been into Italian and Latino arrogant macho men," Dmitri says. "Probably some throwback to my own peacock of a Greek father. I can't get it up over another Greek man; it's just too weird, sort of incestuous, even to imagine. But something about the Mediterranean version of macho has always secretly turned me on. Maybe it's also a kind of backlash against the push I also felt from my mother—to get as far away from those working-class roots as we could. I'd be turned on by garage attendants or plumbers or 'real men' who worked in construction and, while I got involved with this or that 'appropriate' man in college, including two bona fide over-on-the-Mayflower WASP, in my fantasies I was having rough sex with an Italian American dockworker in some dark alley. I hated myself for these fantasies, especially because what really turned me on was the prospect of violent domination. What makes me pop is *danger*. I know I'm not the only gay man with these fantasies—hell, look at the rows and rows of porno tapes with abduction and rape as the theme—and I've actually done some role-play stuff with various Guido types I've met through ads, always secretly, and almost always followed by a terrible descent into guilt. Various late-night trips out to the Bronx, with lots of pot and poppers as well as booze before I got sober. I've really done a number on myself after some of these sex scenes. I can't stand that I can't eradicate these fantasies. They just seem so sick."

Mark has felt similarly bedeviled by his own secret fantasies, which in his case center on college jocks: "I'll see a twenty-one-year-old walk by in shorts and a tank top not having any idea how beautiful he is, and I'll go nuts. Zoloft did have one tempering effect on all this: it drove down my libido to nearly zero, but now that I'm off Zoloft, the old fantasies are coming back and the old yearning to play around with ecstasy and Special к. I just want to surrender to someone—just get taken over. I can't tell you how many times in the past year or two, maybe even more since I met Dmitri, I've wanted to call up my old drug contacts. Following a suggestion our counselor made, I tore up all the old phone numbers of drug dealers. But I can't tear them out of my memory. I remember every single number."

What apparently has made the urge to go back to drugs even more pressing is Dmitri. "I know I'm being a prick when I do this," Dmitri says. "But I never did stuff like ecstasy and к. I'm so jealous sometimes of Mark when he talks about scenes he had when he was high on those drugs. I'll admit it—sometimes I goad him, tell him we should experiment doing that stuff together, that it would probably help our sex lives. They just seem so different to me from getting trashed on booze. Mark and I have really gotten close to saying 'Screw it!' I've watched Mark as he reached for the telephone to call an old dealer more than once. And I've watched him hang up the phone just as quickly. We both instantly feel like assholes. And I feel incredibly guilty for egging him on. But it just seems like such a great solution for us, sometimes."

Mark agrees, but he's adamant in his resolve not to blow his sobriety: "I don't want to go down that hole anymore. Sometimes I scream at Dmitri when he goads me like that. What is he trying to do, kill me? And he shuts down, like a puppy dog who's been kicked. So we try, in and out of therapy, to go the 'talking route' instead. Jesus, we've talked ourselves into oblivion. And it's no secret why we're fixated on so many of the scenes and fantasies we have. I mean, young college jocks obviously represent the kind of 'regular guy' I always thought my father wanted me to be. Since I couldn't be that kind of jock, I guess I just want to have one. But the pursuit seems pretty doomed. It just somehow all makes me more self-hating, makes me feel even more inadequate. The guys that turn me on don't only have to be young and muscular; they have to be dumber than me too. A legacy from my mom, probably. It was so damned important to her to be smart." Mark sighs. "Which is another problem about Dmitri. Dmitri's smart. And while that makes him great to talk to and take home to Mom and Dad as a presentable boyfriend, it's a turn-off. I've felt like I'm just jammed into a dead end. Not only with Dmitri, but with anyone other than one of my fantasy jocks. I really didn't have a clue how to get out of it. Except—and this, thanks-but-no-thanks to Dmitri's seductive encouragement—by going back to the right 'designer drugs.' But, damn, I am not going to do that. Not now. And I hope not ever."

Dmitri was intrigued by Mark because Mark was so different from anyone else he'd ever been involved with, not least because Mark was the first sober man Dmitri had ever been involved with. "In group, Mark kept saying he was looking for a relationship, something that would satisfy him and last longer than the one-night stands that were the only 'romantic' contacts he'd had previously. There was something so, I don't know . . . *comforting* about Mark. I'd just been involved with this crazy older bearded guy who was an artist, perennially in debt, and with whom I had some of the best, most exciting sex I've ever had, but it was all violent role-playing stuff and it just freaked me out. Especially since the guy was always high on pot. I'm amazed I didn't just fall back into doing that with him, but somehow I didn't. But I've just had this incredible desire to be with someone normal, someone with a job, a savings account, someone who dressed preppy. Not the least of it was, I just came out to my father. He was predictably devastated, but his main worry was that I'd end up with some sex-crazed, disease-ridden lunatic and ruin my life. I guess, maybe to placate him but also to placate my own secret fears that I was heading into that hell, I decided to make sure I started meeting people my family would approve of. Mark certainly looks the part, and I liked what he had to say in group—he was smart, sensitive, funny. And so we started to date. I mean, nothing but date. We had some enjoyable dinners, went to the movies; I met some of his friends. But there was no sex. Not even any sexual tension. I was willing to try, but Mark just seemed so shut down. Finally I brought things to a head. I invited Mark over for a 'romantic' dinner and made some moves on him. He just sat there like a lump. I've never been confident about my attractiveness, and I really took it personally. Mark saw how hurt I was, and we started to talk."

Dmitri and Mark knew a good deal about each other's backgrounds and hang-ups from group, but now they tried to go deeper, to really tell each other "the truth." The hurt, the anger, the connections to childhood all slowly came out—first from Mark, then, as Mark turned the tables and asked the same questions Dmitri had asked him, from Dmitri. "I guess we were both bowled over by how much we had locked up from each other. I'd gotten to this point before with lovers—I mean, it wasn't the first time I'd chewed over the conflict I'd always had between the cleaned-up preppy CEO I felt I had to be in my public life and the depraved sexual beast I felt in my private life," Dmitri says. "But I was determined to go further this time. When Mark said he was only able to get turned on by younger guys who were less intelligent or articulate than he was, my first impulse was to blurt out: 'Well, why are you wasting time with me?' But I didn't want to say that; I didn't want to alienate Mark. I knew he was telling me difficult, painful, intimate stuff, and I didn't want to throw it into his face. Then I got an idea."

Mark had confessed that one of the hottest scenes he'd had with one of the young men he'd managed to lure into his bed involved massage. "Nothing heavy-duty. I mean, all I did was get some oil and just work over the guy's body, and it was so sensual, and so satisfying—and so nonintimidating." Dmitri asked Mark to give him a massage, and then they'd switch. "No expectations," Dmitri said. "We don't have to have sex. Let's just try touching each other." Dmitri turned out most of the lights in his apartment, lit some candles, and both men wordlessly stripped. "It was awkward at first," Mark says. "I mean, as much as Dmitri said he wasn't after sex, I didn't really believe him. I was ready to dismiss this as some awful self-help-type exercise you'd find in *Cosmopolitan* magazine. But with the candlelight flickering, and as I started to work the oil into Dmitri's back, I started really enjoying myself. I never realized how smooth and sensual skin could feel. It was just so . . . gentle, satisfying, warm. Dmitri then got on top of me and started touching me in the same gentle, strong way. It was all we did. We fell asleep that night, right there, all greased up. It's strange to make this connection, but it's like we found some natural or organic way to feel as loose as I ever felt on K, but without doing any drugs at all. It was as if I was discovering some capacity to do for myself what I'd had to take drugs for before. By morning, half awake, sleepy, and warm, we had sex, and it was incredible. It was almost like the first real sex I'd ever had—the first sex that felt like an even exchange, anyway. It certainly was the first sober sex I'd ever had."

Since that time, they both decided to join a gym. "Both of us feel terrible about our bodies," Mark says, "which is another thing that unites us. Dmitri keeps thinking he has to turn into some cut-ab version of one of the college jocks who turn me on. I'm as big and lumpy as my father—at least that's how I see myself—and I've always felt like a graceless jerk, even though Dmitri keeps telling me he thinks I'm hot. But somehow just doing something physically with each other—just being gym buddies with each other—is satisfying, almost like that night of massage and rubbing up against each other like sleepy babies was." Dmitri's eyes glint: "We've even started verbally to share some of our sexual fantasies with each other and to explore—just a little—some of the role play we used to be so ashamed of. I guess this is the revelation: we're seeing that we just might be able to give expression to the 'dark' parts of us. Sort of play with our fantasies without getting overwhelmed by them."

The actions that Dmitri and Mark's new awareness have led them to—massage, going to the gym, talking to each other more completely about their fears and fantasies—grow organically out of the feeling of *safety* each now tries to make possible for each other. "A good tip from our therapist is to limit the times we talk about our distress or depression or negative stuff we're feeling about each other," Dmitri says. "This is a whole new way of thinking of problem solving for me. I mean, any distress in my family got chewed over from morning to night, the same accusations hurled at each other again and again until we all just stomped off in a huff and stopped talking to each other. Now Mark—who does tend to be a lot more organized with his time than I do—actually makes appointments with me to talk about stuff that's bothering him. That may seem artificial, but it ends up reinforcing the sense of safety—that we'll be able to contain the difficult stuff—we each want to feel with each other. By setting a time to talk about stuff, we're bringing some structure to what upsets us. We're making it manageable."

Different people implement change in different ways. Mark is used to making lists and following directions; Dmitri is good at the spontaneous insight, letting Mark know what he intuits is going on beneath their words. We've seen in Cris's approach to Maddy that we can learn to talk to each other without it sounding like some kind of fourth-grade homework or fulfilling an AA assignment, like a Fifth Step. Indeed, even with Mark's more regimented approach, there's no doubt in either his or Dmitri's mind that they're both operating from genuine caring. If they weren't, no approach—regimented or free-flowing—would have a chance of working. Finally, as many effective "techniques" as we may find and develop to help reach each other, to help each other hear what's in our minds and hearts, there's something mystical about caring and love. It can't be coerced. We can, perhaps, variously beckon to it—create a context or atmosphere in which our loving (and angry and sorrowful and frustrated) feelings have space to reveal themselves. But the aim is not to impose some predetermined idea of "love" onto ourselves or our partners. It's to help us *hear* without judging and to help us come up with behavioral suggestions we can manageably follow to bring us at least one tiny step closer to a satisfying life. This is not a bad description of the effect of a good Twelve Step meeting: the open-ended listening it often engenders and the down-to-earth, how-to-do-it suggestions you commonly hear in the rooms.

A dividend seems to be that cultivating sober consciousness in this way also tends to widen and deepen our routes to pleasure. It's telling that Mark made the connection to feeling as sensual and loose with Dmitri sober as he once felt only by taking Special κ. Once again, our experiences with getting high end up being instructive—not just as warnings or cautionary tales, but as reminders of the kind of totally immersing pleasure we once sought and were able to find, even if we had to get high to find it. To admit that we still crave that pleasure sober doesn't have to translate instantly into "I still want to do Special κ." By many alcoholics' and addicts' estimations, you're not an addict *unless* you want to do drugs or get high—even in sobriety. It's all right to feel that way—it had better be, since so many of us seem to have no choice but to feel that way! But to hang on, look deeper, see more about *why* we wanted to "get high," what sort of pleasure we wanted to provide ourselves—this can be the beginning of discovering how to provide ourselves with something just as earth-shatteringly pleasurable while *sober*. So many lesbians and gay men have taught me that "sober sex" and "sober love" are far more gloriously pleasurable and fulfilling than the insensible gropes we experienced high on drugs or booze. Once again (Bill W. reminds us whenever we need the reminder): "There is a substitute, and it is vastly more than that."

"Vastly more than that" in this context describes the realm of "real" love—a love grounded in and growing from our deepest desires, a love that (if we can only learn to get out of its way) seems to want to create itself.

## Awake and Dreaming: Achieving "Real" Love in Sobriety

Our sexual and romantic fantasies may sometimes strike us, rationally, as ludicrous, especially in sobriety. Mark knows "rationally" that he can't construct a happy life by searching out one twenty-one-year-old college football player after another or by becoming that perfect college jock himself. But as he explores ways to accept himself more, to indulge in a more satisfying phys-ical life and work on his body with Dmitri, as he puts less stress on "performance" in his sexual relationship with Dmitri, and (es-sentially) *as he finds he can do all this without drinking or drugging,* he is finding—slowly—that he is capable of feeling as good about himself as if he *were* that kid jock. Both Dmitri and he are also discovering that sexual fantasy doesn't have to scare or depress them, now that it lacks the buffer of drugs and booze; they might actually be able to have fun with scenarios that they once labeled taboo or impossible.

Our romantic and sexual imaginations offer us infinite possi-bilities in sobriety, far wider options than the hazed-over sexual ruts we often fell into the moment we got high. We start to enjoy those possibilities sober when we realize that we don't have to fear fantasies, nor do we always have to act on them so literally—very much as we learn we can feel the urge to drink or take drugs and not act on it. There are other ways to satisfy cravings that won't kill us. As we grow in self-acceptance, it becomes more possible to play "pretend"—to have fun even with what we may formerly have labeled our "darkest" thoughts and dreams and visions. Mark and Dmitri continue to learn new ways to help each other feel safe while they make these forays into their secret selves.

"Part of it," Dmitri says, "comes from accepting not only the 'dark' stuff, but the fact that it does turn out to be important to me to be with someone who knows how to act in public. I mean, I will always be my family's child. For example, it turns out that I share some of the same dreams my mother has, and it's okay that I do. I mean, I wouldn't mind living in a *Town and Country* spread myself. I used to think that was superficial. But making money isn't such a bad idea, and having a 'good life' seems like a fine goal. Maybe Mark and I can learn to do both—have a kind of 'normal' life and a playful fantasy life at the same time. Maybe we can be all of who we are. Mark still sighs and shakes his head when I say stuff like this. 'You really think that's possible?' he asks. But, you know, I'm beginning to think it is possible. Not only possible, but something we're actually managing, bit by bit, to make true right now in our lives."

The "sober" in the phrase "sober love" doesn't mean "down-to-earth" or "boring" or imply in any way that we should expect to give up our dreams and our yearnings in a love relationship. It's possible to get beyond the hard facts of what limits us and explore how to make our richest and most exciting dreams come to life. The reality of real love seems to be composed as much of our dreams as it is of our actual day-to-day concerns and experiences. Negotiating a balance between dream and reality comes with practice, my recovering gay friends teach me: new ways of connecting verbally and behaviorally and emotionally can be learned and used—again and again. Cris's realization that the Tenth Step ("Continued to take personal inventory . . .") is not just filler is a realization that now floods Mark and Dmitri as well, even if they don't tend to think in Twelve Step vocabulary terms. But maybe what Cris and Maddy and Dmitri and Mark most teach me is that our private fantasies and cravings and dreams in sobriety deserve as much compassionate and curious attention as we can bring to them. Paying them that needed attention does seem to open doors to newer options, ways of thinking, and prospects of connection than many of us ever thought possible back in the days we drank or drugged. Our stories end up being a testament, from a lot of struggling and hopeful recovering gay men and women, that you can be all of who you are in your relationships and in your life. And that, at least for me, is "vastly more than" I ever thought possible when I was strung out and out of it on booze and drugs.

# 5 Courting Sober Dreams: Finding Meaning in Work

As you begin to function better in sobriety (or recovery, "uncovery," spiritual awakening, rational enlightenment, or whatever you're calling the state of living without drugs and alcohol), as whatever maintenance strategies you've employed to keep yourself physically abstinent become more second nature, something annoying almost always happens. New frustrations and hungers and desires make themselves felt. Perhaps strongest among these is the growing need to feel that what you're doing has meaning. I have never talked to a gay or lesbian recovering alcoholic or drug addict for whom this was not an urgent issue. Few long-term gay and lesbian recoverers have, or are happy having, jobs that merely pay the rent.

There does, after all, seem to be in this arena every bit as spiritual a hunger as Jung and Bill W. suggested underlay our hunger for sex or drugs or booze. It doesn't matter whether you're a staunch AA-goer or are on the fence regarding the Twelve Steps: if you're like every gay recovering person I know, you crave the sense that what you're doing matters.

Job-to-career stories abound in our lives, many of which you undoubtedly have heard or lived out and dreamed about yourself—including those of people who've made quite abrupt departures from what they previously did (a Wall Street broker who becomes a social worker; the commercial artist who begins her own baking business; the fourth-grade teacher who becomes an

AIDS activist), as well as those who've been able to find deeper meaning in the fields in which they already worked.

Maybe the strong tidal pull toward meaningful careers that I see in every lesbian and gay man I've talked to for this book is a product of the more general pull toward finding meaning in our lives. The more I consider Freud's bedrock conditions that have to be satisfied for us to have any chance at happiness—love and work—the more I think it's actually only love. At least, the gay and lesbian recoverers I know continually search for ways to do what they love: there's an ineradicable connection between love and work for us, a connection that is, at first, usually very confusing and full of conflict, a conflict that is often particularly crippling because it's grounded in the secret suspicion that what we love is either sick or silly or inappropriate, and that spending our lives pursuing it would be narcissistic and self-indulgent—or too "gay." So much of what we love is connected to what we were and are told we *shouldn't* love. The gay boy who yearns to dance in a chorus line but whose father wants him to be the next Don Mattingly, the lesbian who wants to be an admiral but whose mother wants her to be the next Mary Tyler Moore—well, that describes cliché versions of the dilemma, but it makes the point quickly.

I've struggled in my own working life with so much of this kind of shame and fear, and not just when I was an active alcoholic. Certainly drinking didn't help the dilemma. Over the sixteen years (from ages eighteen to thirty-four) that I imbibed greater and greater quantities of vodka, alcohol very effectively ate away at my talents, abilities, and self-belief—and especially any secret dream I'd ever nurtured of being a writer. The jobs I took, starting in New York City in the mid-1970s (the heyday of no-holds-barred sex clubs, at all of which I was a regular), began with a few "respectable" entry-level positions in publishing but quickly devolved into a low-level off-the-books office job where

I typed and answered a phone when I wasn't taking three-hour "lunches" at a local Irish bar, fueling up. I wrote some pretty good letters, I'm told (by the faraway friends with whom I spent most of my working hours corresponding, a much more palatable task than the dictation I was supposed to be typing up), but otherwise I was on a downward spiral from which I couldn't imagine ever emerging. I had proved to be completely inept in the "real world" of Getting Ahead in a Career, throwing away papers I was supposed to file, calling in sick whenever I thought I could get away with it, and missing every deadline I was given.

That last miserable off-the-books clerical office job marked my lowest professional point: my self-esteem was zero. My despair had become nearly intolerable by the time, halfheartedly, I somehow got it together to mail out résumés to randomly selected literary agencies (I remember writing that I was willing to sweep floors). Amazingly, I ended up working for a brilliant, lively, somewhat eccentric literary agent who seemed to see me as an *artiste manqué*. My hair and beard were still hippie length (it was 1982) and I wore—day and night—prescription sunglasses, the combined effects of which made me look like I was always in hiding, which indeed I was. I tried to be charming, succeeded at being duplicitous, wrote amusing reports on manuscripts, but basically my life was vodka, which I drank at midday and after work, nursing the misguided notion that as long as I stuck to vodka, no one would be able to smell alcohol on my breath. Of course, when you drink as much of it as I was drinking, it reeks out your pores, a reek so pervasive and encompassing that you grow used to it: you may not know it's there, but everybody else does. The agent I worked for knew, I think, that I was a drunk the moment I walked through the door, but somehow this made me something of a romantic figure to her. (One of her former husbands—the one she'd loved most passionately—had been a drunk too; sometimes

135

I think she saw me as his reincarnation.) Despite most of the evidence, she persisted in believing that there was something in me worth cultivating. Knowing this woman as well as I came to know her, I see now that I must also have seemed to her a project she could "fix"—something she loved doing. I hung on to her hope more than mine, as assistant and then full-fledged literary agent for six years, the first three of which I was drunk, the final three of which were the first three years of my sobriety. Virtually from the first day I walked into her office, she decided that I should be writing books as well as helping her with the agency (those "amusing" manuscript reports had captivated her). Drunk or hungover (I was never anything else), I somehow cranked out the work she was sure I could do. These first books were chameleon-like collaborations with celebrities of various stripes (ranging from Quentin Crisp to Jim Palmer), and I felt amazed, but somehow also miserable, to be doing them.

Why miserable? Wasn't this what I wanted? Allegedly. But it seemed illicit: I was sure I didn't have whatever credentials you were supposed to have to be allowed to write and get paid for it. It all seemed like some kind of sleight-of-hand trick. Surely, eventually, I'd be found out as the impostor I was certain I was. But the "sneaky" sense I had about putting one over on everybody also made this a marvelous and crazy time for me, as long as I kept drinking. I went to publishing parties, played out every jaded "writer" persona I could think of: a crazy game, ultimately doomed to collapse, but I scraped a little glamour out of it while I could. Then my misery deepened to the point that I found myself bursting into tears for seemingly no reason. Even I began to see that something inside was ruining me. More deeply, I was flooded with the growing, gnawing feeling that *I still wasn't writing what I wanted to write*. Although I didn't realize it at the time, my desperation was impossible to assuage as long as I kept drinking. I remember watching a rerun of the old Hitchcock film *Lifeboat,* with Tallulah Bankhead flashing her diamonds in the middle of the Atlantic Ocean and everyone dying of thirst, despite the endless sea around them. I identified completely. I was looking for water in a well where the only available liquid, vodka, was just as toxic as all that salt water around Tallulah.

I finally did stop drinking and, a good year and a half into my sobriety, found that I could once again string sentences together. I began to write more honestly, almost as a matter of course: the course of sobriety. Happily, my recovery fed directly into my work life: because I had less to hide, I seemed to have more to say. I turned the very aspects of self that once caused me the most shame into grist for my all-too-public writing mill—my alcoholism and my sexuality. But the old doubts and self-attacks persisted and sometimes still do. I can still feel very shaky as I attempt to coax more and more of my unconscious mind into consciousness and funnel it into my work. This is scary stuff—in some ways scarier in sobriety because I'm more aware of my fear and anger, fear and anger that I had once fled so effectively through alcohol. I'm now publicly saying and writing self-revealing things that would have horrified me when I started out, back as that drunken *artiste manqué* who stumbled into the literary agent's office. The kicker is, sometimes I'm still horrified at myself, despite my "rational" understanding that there's no reason to be.

I realize now that while I am more than ever an almost literal "open book," and that ultimately the effect in my life of *being* that open book has turned out to be wonderfully, nourishingly liberating, I haven't entirely transcended the old inner sense that I'm being a "bad boy": as if I ought to be punished for being so honest about my life. This sometimes leads to self-sabotage, even in sobriety—finding ways to punish myself when I don't find sufficient punishment coming from other quarters. What my own struggles to be myself in public (or in print) also teach me is that the self-sabotage urge is at least partly homophobic. It's not only a product of my alcoholic fears; it's also a lingering toxic vestige of my fear of revealing myself as gay as well as alcoholic or compulsive. Indeed, "gay" and "alcoholic" and "compulsive" all once seemed (and sometimes still unconsciously seem) synonymous. I still sometimes feel as if I should be punished even for my sober self-revelations: the idea was so entrenched in me to mistrust the topics that compelled me, and it sometimes still rears up and tells me that I should be punished as much for doing what I love as for loving who I love.

This connection—between love and work, that they are each ultimately fraternal twins—seems to me especially inextricable in other gay recovering people I know as well. I see so many instances of subtle self-sabotage in the work arena that reflect the kinds of punishment many of us inflict upon ourselves as a reaction to being gay. I am so grateful to have had someone as encouraging as the literary agent I found, a true catalyst in my career; few of us are blessed with such help. But I am also aware that the responsibility for growing in my career and life very much starts and remains with me: it takes a Tenth Step kind of vigilant inventory taking to make sure that I'm not, in the work arena, once more acting out a kind of self-hate or mistrust—that I'm not secretly or unconsciously trying to "prove" that I'm really a no-good faggot fake and that I not only don't deserve to "succeed," but shouldn't presume to do what I "love."

*It's all right to do what you love.* That was and sometimes still is the hardest pill to swallow—not only for me, but for so many other recovering gay people. Yet, these same people often give me more hope than I'm able to give myself that it might be possible to do what we love. We are an inspiring bunch, perhaps nowhere more than in this job-to-career arena. For example: Jean.

## A Secret Therapist

"Sometimes I try to think what the most liberating moment of life has been so far," Jean muses. "Was it the moment I 'saw the light' and stopped drinking and smoking pot? Was it the moment I first made love to a woman? Was it the moment I actually enrolled in grad school to start getting my master's degree in social work—something I never thought I'd ever do in a million years? Or maybe it was when I opened up my office as a therapist? Surely that was it." Jean laughs.

"Nope. It was when I walked into the den in Clare's house one late Saturday morning, not long ago, and there she was, screaming at the TV with her nine-year-old son, Billy, at these huge men throwing each other around in the ring. Clare is a WWF addict. She loves watching professional wrestling. And when I walked in there and saw how wildly she loved something so 'inappropriate' . . . I don't know. I just lost it. Something came together for me. And this was after I'd struggled through all my self-hate, all the stuff that was keeping me from doing what I wanted to do in my life. This was *after* I thought I'd won most of the battles in my life. But something inside me had never really completely untied. I still had some of the old sneaking suspicion that I was a complete fraud to be 'helping' other people. I was still too sick to be able to do that. And then I see Clare screaming as loud as any of those sweaty galoots on the TV screen. And suddenly . . . I don't know; the world seemed *habitable*. You really *could* do what you wanted to do."

Jean, at forty-five, has had to battle a lot of demons. "My mother was a secret drinker for most of her life. I say 'most' because the secret was out by the time I was sixteen and found her nearly comatose on the kitchen floor one late night when I couldn't sleep and wanted to get something to eat out of the refrigerator. Frankly, I was almost glad she wasn't awake. Because if she had been, she would probably have slapped me hard across the face for getting up and 'stealing' food from the kitchen when I knew how much of a struggle it was for her to make ends meet and feed me and my little sisters on her fixed income and how could I have been so selfish. . . . I didn't know then that what my mother subjected me and my sisters to was abuse. This was before child abuse or battering had become subjects for TV movies. I only know that her first response when she got mad at us was to hit us. I walked around the house as a kid wincing when I heard her footsteps. It was only a matter of time before she'd blow up at us. By the time I was seventeen, my mother was hospitalized and diagnosed as schizophrenic. I don't know about that label, but she certainly was a lunatic—an abusive, violent, horrible lunatic. My sisters and I bonded early on, and I did what I could to protect them. But again, I didn't know it wasn't normal to get punished like my mother punished us. I thought that's what all mothers did. Not that I thought she was normal exactly. I never had a best friend when I was growing up, I think because I was too afraid of how my mother might have behaved if I'd brought a friend home. She was just so angry all the time. I didn't want anything embarrassing to happen in front of anyone. So I just didn't get close to anyone—anyone other than my sisters. Maybe it was my sisters who kept me sane. There was love and affection between me and them, at least."

When her mother was hospitalized, Jean's sisters were informally adopted by her grandmother—"not my mother's mother, but my father's. My dad had died in a car accident years before, probably because of drinking too. *His* drinking wasn't secret, as my mother never tired of telling us. But Grammy kept in touch with us, and she was really quite wonderful when Mama was taken away. She has a big heart. I only wish she could have adopted all of us years before. By that time I was about to graduate from high school. I was already pretty much grown up, at least by chronological age. I think something in my heart of hearts just told me it was too late for me—I'd already been too screwed up by my upbringing to get any real help. But my sisters were still only nine and eleven years old. Maybe they could get 'saved.' As for me, I was a lost cause."

Jean left her hometown in the suburbs of Chicago as quickly as she could for the Big City. "I had always known I was gay. I mean, the only romantic dreams I ever had were always about girls, women. Maybe that's another reason I kept myself from having a 'best friend.' I was afraid I wouldn't be able to hold back what I really wanted to do—take off our clothes and make love. I had these fantasies really early on. It always amazes me when I hear from Clare that she really didn't know she was lesbian until she was in her twenties! That seems incredible to me. How could you not know? I identify with most gay men in this way more than I do with a lot of lesbians. Every gay man I've met says he knew he was gay from his earliest childhood. It was the same with me. But the knowledge just seemed to be one more thing that, if I ever let anyone know about it—and especially if I ever let my mother know about it—would just have labeled me as 'sick.' I couldn't imagine the beating I'd get if I ever told my mother something like that! I really think she might have killed me."

Jean had never had so much as a sip of wine before she moved to Chicago, but within days she was a regular in gay bars and "a total lush. I was pretty, fairly slim—didn't look dykey, especially. I was new meat is what I was. And I got sort of sucked up and passed around from one woman to another to another. Again, I identify more with gay men about this sexual stuff than I do with most women I know. Except that there was always something emotional—I mean, it wasn't just anonymous sex. The best part of going to bed with a woman for me was always the tenderness, the caressing—the *being held*. My only experience of that before had been between me and my sisters, but honestly, that was not sexual—I mean, there wasn't any molestation going on, just hugging. No one had ever expressed this kind of sexual love for me before—or what passed for 'love' in the drunken encounters I kept having in Chicago. I'd get jobs as a waitress between live-in lovers. Lovers with whom the tenderness would almost always turn into abuse. God, when I think how ingenious I was in hooking up with women who ended up being just as violent and abusive as my mother, even when they started out seeming like they were affectionate and tender and warm. It's like I could clue into the violent part, as hidden as it usually was, and *that* was the woman I'd go for. The pattern just went on and on. I had as many black eyes as a young woman in Chicago as I'd had as a little girl in the suburbs. Pot helped. Pot took away from both the physical and the mental pain. For a while anyway. For a while until—it's funny. I was wondering before what the most liberating moment in my life was. Now it occurs to me that the *first* most liberating moment was when I decided, quite calmly, that I'd had enough of everything and it was time to kill myself. Yes, I felt really free then. That was such a relief, that idea. I could just end it all. One last big 'fuck you' to the whole world."

Jean's lover at the time she made this decision was a bartender at an Irish bar—"not a gay bar, either, but a real tough men's bar. She was treated like one of the guys, most of whom she pretty closely resembled. Big tough strong woman, not someone you'd want to meet in a dark alley. She had a supply of Valium in the medicine cabinet that she liked to mix with wine before going to bed; it was the only way she could knock herself out to go to sleep. One night, when she was at work, I swallowed every last pill in the bottle. I can't remember how many, but it turned out to be enough to immobilize me, though not quite kill me, as I discovered when

I woke up the next day in the hospital. My lover had come home, found me on the bedroom floor, and sort of called up an ambulance like she might have called up the Salvation Army to remove a couch she no longer wanted in her living room. It was her way of discarding me more than helping me."

By this dismal point in her life, Jean was almost thirty. "They hooked me up with some sort of social worker—oh God, because I'd tried to kill myself, there was a whole rigmarole I had to go through, all sorts of city and state laws that regulated your life if you were bent on doing yourself in. I was incarcerated in the mental wing of the hospital, had to go to therapy, ended up going to some in-house AA meetings and, as I said, hooked up with this social worker. I'd like to say I 'saw the light' right then and there, but really I was just as depressed as I'd been before I'd emptied that Valium bottle into my throat. This was before Prozac and Zoloft and all that stuff—I think maybe Xanax was starting to get used. I don't know; it's all a blur. They put me on Haldol and then Lithium and in other ways tried to medicate me into some semblance of humanity. But nothing really touched me. It just all numbed me. My social worker did do one useful thing. She got me on welfare and into a small apartment. I felt just like my mother. It was pretty much what happened to her after my father died. Find someplace to file me away . . ."

Jean's new home was a tiny, thin-walled studio in a big faceless apartment building. "You could hear everyone else in the building through the walls, floors, ceilings. But there was one lady on my floor—she reminded me of my grandmother, actually, though she was black and came from Georgia and loved to cook, none of which traits my grandmother shared. She was different in another way—she knew how to play the welfare game. There were so many benefits you could get if you knew how to get them! For some reason she took to me and invited me over for dinner all the time. She always had these incredible sort of smoked-ham stews going, and for the first time in my life, I started to gain weight. I didn't have to worry about holding up my end of the conversation, either; she just rattled on amiably about her cousins in Georgia and the pie she was going to bake the next day and what her social worker had told her that morning and how much she enjoyed going to somebody you could just talk to and did I want another portion of stew or bread or rice pudding or anything? Her social worker kept coming up a good deal. 'I never thought I'd go to a therapist,' she said, 'but it's really been helping me a good deal.' After a while, I realized she was trying to get me to go to one too. She was pretty deft in engineering all this, now that I look back on it. One day she asked me to meet her at her social worker's office to help her do some shopping right after, and it turned out she'd made an appointment for me. I was taking anti-anxiety medication, along with a steady stream of wine and pot, and anything was pretty much okay with me. But it did end up being a turning point."

The "turning point" at first had more to do with what the social worker looked like than anything she said. "I was shocked, even through the fog of medication and pot and alcohol. She looked like a cleaned-up version of my mother. She was who my mother would have looked like if my mother had been sane—that's what I re- member thinking. Pretty, well-tailored, smiling, efficient, kind, smart, funny—all the things you could tell my mother might have been had she not been a total whacked-out lunatic. It was like someone had sort of given me my mother back, new and improved. All of which meant I wanted to talk to her, or rather listen to her, to see if my intuition was right. It was weird. There was something almost science fiction about the connection."

Jean sighs. "She wasn't anything like my mother, thank God— past a superficial physical resemblance. But something clicked with Diane right off and began the process I'm still on. She gave me the Twelve Step slogan line about 'being sick and tired of being sick and tired' very early on and whew! Did that ever make sense to me. I started going to AA and NA meetings and I liked them. I began meeting *sober* women—I was amazed there were any! And I began to find out something very, very strange. When I started to speak at these meetings, various people would walk up to me afterwards and thank me. People would ask me for my phone number. Over the weeks and months and years, I got into this whole world of sponsors and sponsees and service and all the stuff you do when you really get into the program, and I sort of gained this reputation as 'guru.' Everyone wanted me to speak at meetings, tell my story." Jean looks truly baffled. "I can't tell you how weird this was to me, discovering this capacity I had to sort of put pain into words and—evidently—help other people. I began to wonder if maybe I didn't want to do what Diane was doing—get my MSW and start seeing clients. But every time I really thought about it, my mother would loom back up and tell me what a sick idiot I was for even entertaining the idea: '*You* helping anybody? Come *on*.' As irrational as I knew this was . . . I don't know. I couldn't get past it."

Jean did manage to get off welfare and find a job working at a women's health care clinic, where she did mostly secretarial and clerical work, answered the phones, and set up appointments with clients, but this also established her as something of an informal therapist herself. "Clients would start to want to tell their troubles to me, the receptionist—not whatever counselor in the clinic they wanted to see. This strange power that I never seemed to be able to trust I really had kept drawing people to me. Clare was one of these clients. She wasn't in for 'mental health' reasons but because of a stubborn yeast infection she couldn't get rid of. I think we fell in love the first time she walked through the doorway. I know I did. She was slight and athletic but very *female*—I don't know; that seems like a better word than 'feminine.' She was this radiant happy *woman*. She was also, it turned out, married, although in the process of getting a divorce. I despaired of ever hooking up with her: she was obviously straight, wasn't she? And yet, every time she caught my eye . . ."

Clare and Jean talked and fell in love. Clare couldn't imagine why Jean hadn't already investigated programs to start getting some sort of counseling degree: she, too, recognized the gift. "Clare's experience of life had been so different from mine!" Jean says. "She hadn't been abused, for one thing. She hadn't been told she couldn't do what she wanted to do. That she'd be sick if she even tried to do it. But she somehow got me to apply to a special college deal that got you into an MSW program quickly, to enroll, get accepted, get scholarship money, and—this was about a year later—move in with her while I went to school. Move in with her and her little boy, who was then only about two. Suddenly, I was a kind of co-parent, a college student, and a lover—the lover of a 'normal' woman. How did all this happen?"

Jean pauses and takes a much-needed deep breath. "Well, I've told you the rest. I got the degree and opened my practice and, recently, walked into the den, and there Clare was yelling at all these wrestlers. And I thought, *Wow.* You really can do what you want to do. You can love anyone you want to love, love doing whatever you want to do. You can even get off on something as violent—I reminded myself, *mock* violent—as these wrestlers in the ring. You can fantasize about anything and think anything and dream anything. And you won't get slapped across the face. You know, AA promises you a life beyond your wildest dreams. Turns out they weren't lying." A loud blare issues forth from the TV in the den, outside of which we sit: testosterone-soaked screams to "kill the bum!" waft out over our heads.

"Have you ever heard anything more beautiful in your life?" Jean asks me.

## The Importance of Being Clueless

For someone who experienced the kind of abuse Jean experienced as a girl and young woman to get to a point of thinking that "Kill the bum!" is a beautiful bit of background noise makes vivid the *transformational* quality of change that can—and does—happen for so many of us when we allow ourselves to tolerate our own dreams and desires in sobriety without dismissing them. Coming out and accepting the fact that we need help to stop or alter addictive behavior give us a huge model and enlightening experience of transformation and change. Negotiating our way through love and sex *sober* also slams us into some pretty big turnarounds. But allowing ourselves to pursue what we truly want to do often requires a more subtle process of self-acceptance—and self-celebration. So much seems to devolve into "getting out of your own way," a phrase and a thought that so many women and men we've met in this book have spontaneously pressed onto us as the best and most effective strategy they've learned to employ—in every realm of their lives. But it also means learning to *love* yourself in a way that rams you into whatever homophobia may still be lingering internalized in your gut. The self-mistrust that led us to be so adept at duplicity, at sniffing out ulterior motives in people, of being able to see beneath the surface, developed, as I've suggested, as the result of a great and horrifying wound—a maiming of spirit that told us we were fundamentally sick, loathsome, despicable, unacceptable. We are, I believe, so thoroughly and unconsciously saturated with this notion that even later on, after we've come to some sort of peace with our sexuality, after we've experienced the miracle of recovery, our reflex will still be to mistrust what we love. Sometimes voices even in recovery will subtly and perhaps unwittingly reinforce this sense of self-mistrust: "Beware of what you love! Beware of pleasure! If you indulge yourself too much, you'll get sucked back down the drain of addiction. . . ." We don't realize how important it is to *love* what we love. Although it may seem like a "danger" warning when our self-conscious egos start worrying about "what other people will think" of us, we find that when our "loves" are followed without defensiveness with childlike curiosity, they offer us at least a potential doorway into even deeper and more satisfying sobriety. Getting out of our own way—keeping away from sabotaging ourselves as we pursue our dreams—is sometimes a much stickier process than we realize, even after we've put down that glass, needle, pipe, or pill bottle.

How we accomplish that—"get out of our own way"—is the product of so many paradoxes. Remember Stan, after he'd had his first DF/VD correspondence on the Internet in which "VD" made it clear (in no uncertain terms) that he was "clueless" about sex and sobriety and self-acceptance—and how the acceptance of being "clueless" made him feel simultaneously that he wanted to go to sleep and that he'd just woken up?

There's something in that paradox that strikes a bell for so many recovering gay men and lesbians who've tried to turn their career dreams into reality: it's somehow the paradox of real consciousness. We suddenly know we don't know anything, and yet what we *do* know is more valuable, "smarter," more useful than the contents of any encyclopedia or doctoral degree. We know what it is to feel *alive*. We're "clueless," maybe, but curious. We know what it is to feel life—at least for the moment—without impediment. We know that our ancient self-hating assumptions—that who we are and what we love are unacceptable—are profound lies. We can free ourselves to enjoy the real rewards of sobriety—

the ability to accept ourselves freely, in the moment, without judgment, with delight in what we love, with awe about the much we don't know—at any moment we want to. The key is to let go of any rigid notions we may have at any moment about who or what we have to deal with, and to reconnect with the wonder of being alive and conscious. The key is to love the gifts of this consciousness—the MSW degree that sobriety may enable you to earn, the solo cabaret gig you may now be able to land, the book you may now be able to write—but not to confuse those gifts with real success, which we now know is simply *living consciously*. They are infinite and quite wonderful dividends, the natural byproducts of something far more basic, fundamental, and infinitely fertile: consciousness. I still cannot think of a better definition of sobriety than "consciousness." I still cannot think of a better route to self-acceptance and self-realization than finding ways to enhance consciousness, not just for the wild and amazing bunch of people recovering gay men and lesbians turn out to be, but for any human being on the planet.

That the surest route to consciousness seems to start with what AA calls "surrender" and "humility" and "turning it over" is initially bewildering to many of us: it's a paradox that goes against so much of our cultural and family training, so many of whose operative verbs—*assert*, *debate*, *win*, *intimidate*, *resist*, *strain*, *push*—have such opposite connotations. But, as Grace would probably say if you found her at an AA meeting and asked her what she thought about humility, "It's the best way to get smart." As Adam would probably tell you if you asked him, however, "*Humble* has too much church baggage in it. I think a better word is *clueless*."

This was a hard lesson for thirty-seven-year-old Ben to learn—Benjamin from Boise, Idaho; Ben, the quiet second son of a God-fearing Methodist family for whom Boise was quite "big city" enough. "When I went to college at NYU, I met someone, Peter, who'd managed to get out from under his Amish family's thumb and who was as shell-shocked as I was to be in Manhattan. We seemed to have had just as much trouble convincing our families to let us go to college in the big, bad city. We both were a little battle-scarred, even as freshmen. I found out only much, much later on that he was gay; after we graduated, he wrote me a letter. But that was okay. I didn't even know I was gay until after college. I mean, all the guys I meet say they always knew they were gay, but I really didn't call myself that until I was about twenty-five. All I knew was, I was 'different.' Anyway, from the start of meeting this guy, I felt I had at least some kind of soul mate in the big city. Funny that he had to be Amish for me to relate to him, but it gives you a clue how sheltered I was."

Peter and Ben became friends also because they had each harbored an intense interest in politics—"not the usual kind of stuff, like caring who was going to be elected mayor or congressman or president, but more of a utopian interest in sweeping political change. We both loved reading Marx and were interested in socialism, still believing somehow that it could be instituted without turning into the kind of corrupt and inhuman regimes that versions of socialism had turned into in, say, Russia or Cuba or mainland China. We were theorists, I guess. Anyway, we both ended up majoring in poli sci, although it didn't have much impact on our careers. Peter eventually got some education courses under his belt and taught in elementary school after college. I ended up getting a good job in a big insurance company. But secretly we'd go to Socialist Worker Party meetings together and dream of the day when everyone would be 'equal.'"

Ben laughs. "It's such a code for me, now, looking back—I was aching for a world that would accept me for whatever it was I was. Again, while I knew I was attracted in some vague way to men, I also had had some relationships—even sexual relationships—

with women. I guess I was attracted to many of the renegade socialist groups because they attracted such a wide and wild group
of men and women, some of whom struck me as, say, 'ambiguous'—you couldn't tell if they were straight or gay. One of these
guys belonged to something he called the Radical Faeries, and I
noticed that most of the political people in the socialist party
snubbed him. There was a lot of homophobia in that group, despite its outward diversity. I felt for the guy, even though I learned
he was gay (I'd never heard of the Radical Faeries before this and
was stupid or naive enough not to have clued into what 'Faerie'
meant at first), and started talking to him. I liked him a lot—he
was everything I wasn't: spontaneous, funny, fully 'out' as a gay
man, and determined to live a life that was consonant with his
political beliefs. He lived on almost no money, did some sort of
half-volunteer social work thing, lived in a commune with
mostly gay men and lesbians, and was, as I said, very active in the
Radical Faeries. For some reason, I couldn't get him out of my
mind. I already felt like a hypocrite working for The Establish-
ment in my insurance job, even though I did really well and was
promoted on a regular basis. But I felt like I ought to have been
working for The Movement every moment of my waking life. I
just felt guilty and divided."

Ben says he felt even more guilty and divided when, after
agreeing to attend a Radical Faerie meeting, he found himself
drawn even more to his Faerie mentor, who called himself Robin
because it was such a sexually ambiguous name. "Robin had a
squiggly sort of beard and a lean dancer's body, and he moved like
a dancer too—everything about him seemed determinedly on-
the-fence: he was neither male nor female, but liked 'gender fuck'
costumes, which he always wore to Radical Faerie meetings, like
a sarong that displayed his hairy chest but otherwise looked like
it belonged on Dorothy Lamour. He also—along with many of his

151

cohorts—loved smoking pot. And I discovered I loved smoking pot too."

It was "under the influence" that Ben had his first sexual experience with a man—Robin. "I remember calling Peter up after I went to bed with Robin. It was such a shock, I needed what I knew would be some sort of reality check—don't forget, Peter had had my kind of upbringing as well as my political vision of the world. I needed to know what he thought of me doing this. I let Robin fuck me, and it was like the pot—I loved it from the first moment. I discovered, overnight, in my mid-twenties, not only that I was probably 'gay,' but that I loved being fucked, which to my mind was still horrifying—not only something my father would have found a Methodist abomination, but something I associated totally with being a woman. The androgyny that Robin seemingly had so easily accepted was a much harder pill for me to swallow. The only way I could reconcile any of this was just to get more stoned. That's the state I called Peter up in—stoned. At first he was horrified when he heard what had happened, but then he kept asking for more and more details about the experience, and I got a strong inkling he was gay too, although he didn't say it at the time. But he basically gave it his utopian political blessing. He felt it was just me being a 'comrade' with another 'comrade' and that old notions of gender and sexuality had to change every bit as much as economic assumptions and practices had to change. So it became politically correct for me to have sex with Robin. Later I found out that Peter had another motive—although he couldn't bring himself to do the same thing, he wanted it vicariously, by hearing about the sex. In other words, without my knowing it, I was turning poor Peter on with my stories about Robin and me in bed."

The division between this weekend Radical Faerie self and the very conservative heterosexual atmosphere at his job rankled terribly in Ben, especially as his twenties turned into his thirties and he noticed that people had stopped asking him when he was going to get married. "I got paranoid that co-workers were nudging each other when I was out of sight—that they somehow 'knew' I was gay. My boss had already pegged me as the one to send on business trips, as if he knew I wouldn't have a family to worry about. Another clue, I thought, that he knew I was gay. All this did was make me more stilted and distant at my job. I never had anyone I could call a real friend there; I simply went in and worked, sort of gritting my teeth through the whole thing. I couldn't wait to get away, as I did on weekends, back to Robin and his Radical Faeries, back to sex and pot and a basically unreal feeling that this 'Utopia' we kept on talking about could be somehow brought about if only we wished hard enough for it."

Ben is also aware that his business success was his only way of attracting any kind of acceptance, if not admiration, from his distant family in Idaho. "All my family and I ever talked about was my work, as if there were some tacit agreement not to talk about anything else. It was like the part of my life I really cared about— the sex, the pot, the politics—grew larger and larger and more unwieldy, more difficult to keep hidden. But I kept hiding it. When I had vacation time, I'd go on Radical Faerie retreats or hand out pamphlets on behalf of my socialist party. This felt like a relief, but it just worsened how strangled I felt at work. Then Robin and I broke up. Another Radical Faerie suggested that, with the intensity of that experience, I might want to consider tripping on acid with him. God—what a suggestion! But the guy who asked me was someone very popular in the Radical Faerie community, and I was flattered by his attention. I said okay, and we tripped together on LSD. I ended up in a mental hospital—that's basically all you need to know about that nightmare."

In the course of his stint in the mental hospital, Ben was given various blood tests, and it emerged that he was HIV-positive. "Evidently Robin had had a lot of promiscuous sex with no protection. It never occurred to me to use a condom—that's how out of the sexual loop I was. I just couldn't imagine that anyone as philosophically 'pure' as Robin would ever get AIDS. I can't imagine why, now; it seems incredibly stupid to me. But there you have it. Or there I have it—not only AIDS, but another thing to keep from my family."

Once he came down from his trip, people at the hospital strongly urged Ben to attend an in-house NA meeting, since in his whacked-out reverie all he could talk about was wanting to smoke pot, which he associated with comfortable feelings and poignant memories of Robin. Ben did so and found another group where he could be himself—something for which he was always looking. "But the anonymity deal about NA just made it seem like, here was one more thing I had to hide. I began getting really depressed. So depressed that I actually called in sick to work when I got out of the hospital, something I'd never done before. I felt nobody loved, understood, or knew me in any way at all, and here I was with a terminal disease on top of it. I planned to kill myself with pills—met with a psychiatrist and tried to get a big prescription for Valium. He gave me a prescription for Prozac instead, which actually helped—brought me back to some kind of at least tolerable even keel. I got a sponsor in NA, tried to talk a bit more about the split I felt my life had become, felt a little less alone, and began a combination holistic, nutritional, and protease inhibitor program to deal with my HIV. Life seemed a little possible again, but it was certainly no joy."

At about this time, Ben's sister Margaret came to visit. "She brought her little boy, Andy, who was about six years old and got into everything. I have a fairly large apartment in Brooklyn Heights, and I could put them up. But I got absolutely paranoid about little Andy rummaging through my drawers and cabinets and finding all my HIV medicine and enema paraphernalia, which I used for my periodic holistic 'cleansings.' I was terrified that all this might come out in the open, that Margaret would learn things I was sure would terrify her and make her hate me. I tried to pack away anything questionable. I'd told her I was vegetarian, so I knew I could at least carry that off without too many questions. But I was so tense."

Right on cue, not a half hour after a bewildered Margaret (who had never been to New York City before and was visibly stunned by its size and noise and seeming unnavigability) arrived at his apartment, little Andy burrowed into some pile or other and retrieved a pamphlet Ben had somehow missed. "Mommy," Ben says Andy asked Margaret, "what's a hiv?" Margaret said she didn't know, unless Andy (who had just begun to read) meant "hive." "No," Andy said, "it doesn't have an 'e.' It says 'hiv.'" And then he handed Margaret the pamphlet whose title read "Living with HIV."

"Margaret was two years younger than I, and I had always sort of looked out for her," Ben said. "My older brother didn't want to have anything to do with us—he went away to boarding school and college and got away from the family as quickly as he could. Margaret and I were sort of Hansel and Gretel left behind. We became very close, although we didn't talk much. We just spent a lot of time together. But no one in our family had learned to talk about the 'difficult stuff.' We just ignored it. Now, however, Margaret—who after all was no longer a little girl, but a grown woman of thirty—demanded to know what was going on. Was I sick? She barraged me with questions—with Andy there! I couldn't believe this change. It just wasn't something anyone in my family had ever done before. Faced the problem head-on like this, and talked about it."

She saw how uncomfortable I was, and she said, "Do you

know you never talk about your life? I feel so lonely sometimes—the one brother I loved the most, and I can't get him to talk to me. Well, you damned well better talk to me now. Because I care about you."

"Damned" was a shock coming from Margaret's lips, Ben said, "but it had the welcome effect of breaking ice that had never been broken before in our family. Andy just sat there going through some box of magazines I was throwing out—I'd been careful in that instance to weed out the porn and the politico stuff. He had no idea what we were talking about. It was just grown-ups talking, to him. But slowly, I began to tell Margaret about my health and about my struggle to reconcile who I was discovering I was—both sexually and politically—with my 'public life.' Margaret just sat there, transfixed. 'I'm so proud of you,' she finally said. 'Nobody else in our family has ever gotten out of Idaho before! Look at the life you have! I'm terrified that you have the AIDS virus, but you tell me your numbers are good and that you're taking care of yourself. You don't know I had a bout with drinking and then mononucleosis after college—I was weak as a dishrag and couldn't stop drinking through the whole thing. I've gone to some AA meetings myself. But I never told anybody. You don't know how you're helping me by telling me this."

Ben says he knows this sounds "almost too good to be true," and indeed, in some ways, sometimes, he regrets having spilled out everything to Margaret so quickly. "She's as much of a control freak as I am," Ben says. "She started trying to take care of me according to her own fiercely held beliefs about health and diet, and we butted heads a number of times during her visit. But the thing was, I'd let all this out to someone in my family. The repercussions of that . . . well, I'm still feeling them now."

One of the arenas in which Ben is "still feeling them now" is his career. "Not long after this outpouring, and with the help of my sponsor in NA and the support of my more reliable friends in the Radical Faeries, I started to cut back at work—I could do a lot on my laptop at home, and the strain of trying to appear 'straight' or 'normal' was really undercutting my immune system. I started to get a little more friendly with people at work I thought I could trust, actually came out to one co-worker who didn't seem at all fazed by the information. I still haven't told them I have HIV, but that's really none of their business. But the bigger thing is, I've started to 'come out' not so much as a gay man but as a political man. I've started to have discussions about economics and politics with my co-workers at lunch. Sometimes I feel like a secret revolutionary, only less secret than I felt before. It may not seem like much—bringing out what interests me in the work arena—but it's a huge leap for me. I'm now even thinking of an early retirement, where I can do some research on Trotsky I've been wanting to do, travel around to different communes in the country, and basically give more of my energy to what I love. I don't know how this has happened, except to say that staying away from drugs—specifically from the dreamy distant way pot would make me feel—has led to a kind of slow opening in me. Margaret now is one of my best friends. Even she agrees that it doesn't make sense to foist all this on the rest of my family, especially my dad, who seems to be coming down with Alzheimer's right now and probably wouldn't understand much of what I was telling him anyway. But I'm a little bit less alone now. And I feel a little bit less divided. My world isn't split into two parts anymore. While it's not quite one seamless whole, I don't feel as much like one part of me is eternally at war with another part of me."

Releasing more of his "self" into his public and private lives has also made the prospect of "helping people" a good deal less distant than it was when Ben could only conceive of "help" as an abstract philosophical point in a political argument. "I no longer

think so much in terms of 'the good of the people.' I've got a couple of sponsees in NA right now, and what I try to do for their
'good' is a lot more hands-on and simple than adhering to some
kind of Marxist ideology. They need to talk? I listen. They need
help moving a couch? I help them move the couch. They need
someone to go to a movie with so they won't go to a bar or to
their drug dealers? I go to a movie. It's a lot more practical now. I
feel a lot more connected and a lot less hard on myself for not
having created some perfect 'career' that will change the world.
All I have to do is stay sober and stay awake, and the rest seems
to be taking care of itself."

Ben's increased comfort with himself makes vivid the lack of
such comfort so many other gay men and lesbians admit to feeling. "It really is true that we tend to mistrust, even fear, what we
love," he says. "There's the computer analyst I know who really
wants to be an avant-garde filmmaker but who was told his whole
life how 'faggy' the arts were, so he sort of sneaks in working on
his films on stolen weekends. Then there's the lesbian who
wanted to teach math but was told by her family that math—
which her father taught on a college level—just wasn't something
women did or could do. Those are just some of the obvious examples. But I also see really successful people doing terrific
work—who suddenly sort of implode. Like this wonderful writer
I met who did some of the top TV comedy shows and was sought
after by everyone—and, even in sobriety (he'd been sober in AA
for sixteen years), started self-destructing. It was triggered by the
death of his father, which even he thought would release him to
do still funnier and more 'out there' stuff, but it brought on this
huge episode of self-punishment instead. He said he felt somehow
that his career had killed his father, irrational as even he knew
that was. He started missing deadlines. He fell into a horrible
funk. It was like he saw his whole career as this fragile bubble he

had somehow managed to blow without blowing up. But it was only a matter of time before that bubble burst—and it was bursting now. It's like so many people feel almost predestined to fail, even when they've quite obviously succeeded."

This isn't the case with all of us, but it hammers in my point—the painful point that we benefit in sobriety not only from learning to be more comfortable as sexual and social beings but also from learning to accept what we love to do as okay, not one more bit of evidence that we're unacceptable. "I even sing 'Over the Rainbow' sometimes, on the street, out in public," Ben laughs. "You wanna stereotype me? Go ahead."

# 6 A Look at Relapse: The Courage to Change Again

*Relapse* is a frightening word to most people who hear about it or are warned about it in Twelve Step programs. It's as rampant a problem for lesbians and gay men as it is for the "general" population, but I think we (lesbians and gay men) may suffer a particular kind of disillusionment that leads to relapse, a fiercer sense of disappointment, perhaps, than is typically felt by someone whose sexuality hasn't been labeled "contemptible."

I've already suggested that our cravings seem to be so fierce at least partly because deep down we think of them as sick, even those yearnings not obviously a product of our sexuality. The previous chapter about work and sobriety was evidence of my claim that work for many of us is a species of love: most of us are only really satisfied when we allow ourselves to do what we love as well as love whom we love. The seemingly irrational episodes of self-sabotage we create in our lives even in sobriety seem to me, once again, to be attached to internalized proscriptions against doing *anything* "pleasurable"—which can seem to so many of us to be as "sinful," "sick," or "immoral" as we've been told our sexuality is.

It's striking what different connotations the various forms of the word *compulsion* call up. "Can't get him out of OTB? Ah—hell of a compulsion, gambling" gives you the usual force of the noun. "The book really compelled me—I couldn't put it down" or "What a compelling artist Rembrandt is!" give you the force of the verb and adjective. *Compel* and *compelling* often constitute two of our highest terms of praise, and *compulsion* one of our direst diagnoses. Yet they are forms of the same word, and I suggest, in many gay men and lesbians, they unconsciously provoke some of the same fears and self-mistrust. It's interesting that neither word implies a necessarily greater or more focused energy than the other: Michelangelo feeling "compelled" to create a painting on the ceiling of a chapel in the Vatican is arguably as full of tunnel-vision purpose, energy, and desperation as a Bowery bum scrounging around for change for a pint at dawn, at noon, at sundown, at midnight, and then at dawn again. Neither the drunk nor the artist will rest till he gets what he wants. And what each "wants" is to satisfy a desperately felt need—however "exalted" or "depraved" we may decide to label one need or the other.

The men and women who speak to you in this book have had to confront the baffling, painful truth that equivalents of both Michelangelo and the Bowery bum exist simultaneously in themselves. In fact, every gay man and lesbian I've talked to who's battled addiction has acknowledged that the equivalents of both have *always* existed simultaneously—before and after they stopped drinking and drugging. They know that the same person who sneaks into the basement "compulsively" to drink from a hidden bottle of scotch or scurries out into the night to pick up a prostitute may also spend long "compelling" stretches of daylight time in the lab poring microscopically over various DNA helices in his search for an AIDS cure, or making sure each twelve- and thirteen-year-old kid in his or her special ed remedial class gets help and feels cared for. An equally driven energy may well attend both "compulsive" and "compelling" pursuits; a similar quality of passion (hard to tell sometimes from desperation) may characterize both at the outset, however "good" or "bad" we label the outcome.

As I've suggested, the crucial reason so many recovering gay men and lesbians are able to accept the warring but simultaneous existence of "compelling" and "compulsive" in their own psyches comes from having had to accept both dark and light aspects of their dreams, fantasies, and primal cravings in their own lives. We understand—even generally have compassion for—the Jekyll/Hyde splits that fundamentally characterize and confuse so many human beings. Ambivalence is not news to us, because we've spent our lives having to make some sort of peace with our own ambivalences in order to survive. But "ambivalence" continues to shock most of the rest of the world: the Jekyll/Hyde myth has as much terrifying power today as it did for its first Victorian readers. We still live in a world frightened of a good half of its own "primal" drives and desires.

The damage caused by this terror is insidiously crippling and pervasive (alas, the stifling moralism it breeds stains a lot of well-meant recovery literature today). Our still prevalent cultural moral push to pigeonhole motives as either "good" (riveting, engaging, compelling) or "bad" (desperate, self-annihilating, compulsive) *is* damaging not so much because of the content of what's on either side of the good/bad fence, but because of the very imposition of the *split* between those "contents." Any dismissal or automatic judgment signals, to me, a refusal to explore something that terrifies us—in this case, what may link the yearnings at the heart of our most shameful debauches to the motive force behind our proudest accomplishments. (What Stan's sponsor told him, "We're only as sick as our secrets," diagnoses the *secrecy*—the fear that makes us hide our secrets—as sick, not necessarily the content of the secret itself.) We cannot see this link if we are too afraid to open our eyes to see it. Again, I think of the meaning of AA's Fourth Step, which calls for a fearless analysis not a moralistic self-excoriation, and how essential some process of *fearless seeing and assessing* is to the achievement of any kind of satisfying life, not just a "sober" life (a life without alcohol or drugs). Remember from Stan's definition (via VD) of the word, that *fearless* doesn't mean *brave* (standing up to fear); it's a state in which fear has been eradicated. We are much more used to compartmentalizing fear than facing it, tolerating it, exploring it, and ultimately "understanding" it into benignity. Just as grabbing for a shot glass of Schnapps may be a short-term "easier" way of dealing with anxiety than tolerating the anxiety, reflecting on it, and talking about its effects with other people you trust, dismissing fear—"putting it in its place," attempting to "eject" it by ignoring it or diagnosing it simplistically—is a doomed pursuit, as we always eventually find out.

"Jekyll and Hyde" may be as compelling an archetypal tale today as it was when it first appeared in 1879 because we still have not moved much past the essentially Victorian system of moral organization it first codified metaphorically. Victorians certainly had long known the Beast (indeed, pruriently slavered over newspaper depictions of it, only months after the first publication of *The Strange Case of Dr. Jekyll and Mr. Hyde,* in accounts of "Jack the Ripper"), but in his archetypal tale of "good" doctor and "evil" madman inhabiting the same body, Robert Louis Stevenson nudged his readers into an appalling realization from which most of the world has still not recovered: "the Beast" was not only somewhere in the East End dismembering prostitutes; it lurks within our own tightly corseted, determinedly virtuous selves. On the surface this may seem to have been nothing new: for as long as there's been "moral" literature we've had examples of devil-on-one-shoulder, angel-on-the-other inner tugs-of-war. But before Dr. Jekyll mixed up and drank his id-releasing potion, choosing to follow the "angel" promised to eradicate the devil. Not so in Jekyll/Hyde: as hard a grip as Jekyll eventually attempted to keep on his socially acceptable, virtuous self, he could not keep Hyde from breaking in and wreaking havoc. Victorians were introduced to the notion that we might sometimes be powerless over the eruption of our own "dark" drives. No prayer, no force of simple faith, no churchly intervention or absolution seems equal to the task of keeping Hyde completely at bay. He is simply an inevitable and an ineradicable part of the mix. This was news—and very frightening news.

It's also what makes the framing of Jekyll/Hyde's moral dilemma so stunning, what marks it as an authentic paradigm shift (a symbol of the zeitgeist that made Freud possible), a potent myth to which our society, even 120 years later, still anxiously subscribes. Our solution to this dilemma hasn't changed much, either. When Victorians saw in Jekyll/Hyde's cautionary tale the terrible chaos they could unleash if they let the Beast take over, they could think of only one recourse: tighten the corset. Make sure the Beast is *really* locked up. This corset-tightening accounts for much of the essentially fearful moralistic tone we continue to hear today—in and out of AA meetings.

While Stevenson did us a service by constructing a myth that allowed us to understand the Beast as internal (not some bogeyman "out there")—to recognize that he resided *in us*—he also quite dramatically reinforced and intensified most people's fear of the Beast. And therein lies the problem and toxicity of the myth. His unhappy revelation resulted in our being afraid of ourselves, of the volatility of our own inner natures. This fear led to the damaging division we've been exploring throughout this book: the split between sensual, violent, amoral, selfish traits held automatically to be "evil" and an altruistic higher "soul"/self held automatically to be "good." Once again, the fear and self-mistrust that keep the split in place haven't really changed much. (*Jekyll and Hyde* was one of 1997's biggest Broadway musical hits.) We urgently need a new, more embracing—more illuminating—myth about the Beast, especially in the realm of recovery. It's as if we've been stuck in kindergarten for most of our human cultural history, and even such brilliant teachers as we've had haven't been able to get us to advance to first grade.

But what you've seen in these pages are examples of men and women who are advancing to first grade, even if they largely have to teach themselves when they get there. They *are* changing their perception of their "inner" and "outer" personae—widening their views of what's "good" and "bad" in their natures—with immense, in fact incalculable, benefit. Part of that benefit is the discovery that they can stop truly self-destructive *behavior* while at the same time accepting, sometimes even welcoming and embracing, every single thought, fantasy, dream, and wild speculation that pops up in the circus of their minds. Maybe they—*we*—are the rest of the world's first-grade teachers. At any rate, the example of recovering gay men and lesbians beckons to me to put down my crayons and start learning to spell. The beckoning has power not least because I know it comes from people who learned their lessons the hard way: in hell.

Understanding what happens in what we label "relapse" or in other behaviors we may resort to "compulsively" even if we manage to stay away from drugs and alcohol requires exploring the nature of that "hell"—and how getting out of it depends on more than a rote recital of Twelve Step slogans, Steps, or the Serenity Prayer. Getting out of it requires (once again) acknowledging that the "good intentions" with which our particular roads to hell may have been paved were, in fact, *good*: in every bottle of gin, every snort or blow of cocaine, every "bump" of crystal meth or "Special к," *we sought freedom of self*, even if, in practice, what we found (or caused) was obliteration of self. Ultimately *we need to cherish our motives*, not banish some as "Hyde" and clutch fearfully onto others as "Jekyll." However desperately, misguidedly, or "compulsively" we may react to our desires—our cravings—they hold the key to finding out what we really want, and thus who we really are. "Compelling" must reconcile with "compulsive" for us to achieve any kind of peace with either one. We need, in other words, to *understand the connection* between the desperate "compulsive" lunge for freedom/escape of the *spiritus* that we gulped out of a shot glass and the more dedicated, conscious application of will to the pursuit of a deeper, wider, and stronger *Spiritus* that enables us to realize our deepest loves and highest, freest, most "compelling" aspirations.

Shane's story gets to the heart of one "hell" that she couldn't leave completely merely by putting down the bottle: her recovery required some particularly painful soul-searching that certainly has resonance for me—and I expect will reach you too. Her story teaches us something about what's going on when our fears won't let up even after we make demonstrable strides in "recovery"—what happens when we "relapse," what happens when we find ourselves, fearfully, once again grabbing for the compulsive fix rather than the compelling solution.

## Shane

Hell, for Shane, had its roots in never being able to fit who she was into any notion (picked up from school, friends, family, and whatever country she happened to be in) of who she was supposed to be. That Shane is named Shane has a colorful history that gives her own history in a nutshell. She is, first of all, with her athletic reedlike body, golden skin, and dark (compelling) almond eyes, an extraordinarily lyrical mixture of ethnicities: half African (her father was born in Nigeria), one-quarter Chinese, and one-quarter Mexican (her mother). Adding to the mix, her

Chinese Mexican mother was brought up in New Orleans but met Shane's father in Paris where she was a student at the Sorbonne (junior year abroad from Vanderbilt); her father made his living teaching the violin and playing in orchestras. Dumbstruck with love, her mother dropped out of college, stayed on in Paris, married her beloved black violinist, and shortly thereafter, Shane was born. Determined to impose something of her own American citizenship on her infant daughter, Shane's mother insisted on calling her Jane. But the French can't (or won't) pronounce a hard "J" sound, so it always came back at them "Jhayne." Shane therefore grew up thinking Jhayne was her name, and—strong-minded girl as she was even at five—when she was told how she was supposed to spell it, she refused. She wrote "Shane" instead.

"At first, when I was five and began to soak up French and English spelling, I wrote it 'Shayne' in honor of Jayne Mansfield, who had just been killed in a car crash. I liked the irony of it—big buxom Jayne M. was about as far from skinny breastless 'Shayne' as you could get. But that didn't last long. I took out the 'y' and turned it back into one of those androgynous names that lesbians often seem to have or take on—like Robin or Chris—which is maybe, even at five, another reason I wanted to replace Jane with something more ambiguous. I already knew I didn't fit into any of the cubbyholes my own background and upbringing seemed to offer me: I wasn't French, African, Mexican, Chinese, or American, and I didn't feel like any version of male or female I saw around me, either. I was a singular being, sprung out of a mold God had never used before and hasn't used since. Anyway, that's the way I felt when I was little and it's the way I feel now."

Shayne's mother took her back to the States when she was fourteen, allegedly to escape her "male chauvinist womanizing" father. "I was born in 1962, and by 1976, the 'Women's Lib' movement had had its effect even in France, and my mother saw herself suddenly as repressed by patriarchy or something. It all seemed like nonsense to me. My father may have had his 'sexist' ideas about male and female roles, but he turned his back on my mother because she was a drunk. He started having affairs when I was about five or six, I think—at least, that's the earliest time I can remember my mother drunkenly complaining about him. She told me the most intimate details of her past sex life with my father and speculated in equal detail about what his sex life probably was with this or that mistress he took up with. It had one effect on me: I had a horror of sex and a horror of the mess my mother always became every night when she hit the Beaujolais. The French don't really believe in 'alcoholism.' It's an embarrassment to them. It's virtually unpatriotic not to be able to drink moderately in France—you're thought of as unbelievably weak and sick if you can't. But since my mother was to all our French friends and neighbors such a weird mix of nationalities, she was just viewed as an oddity. I was her dumping ground: she told me everything, way before I should have heard it all. I loved her and I hated her. My father just saw me as an extension of my mother—as alien to him as she was. My mother taught me to hate him, and I did. As well as hate everything he did and loved—the violin, music, the whole bit."

Moving back to New Orleans and then to Philadelphia, where her mother's sister had moved, was, Shane says, a culture shock, but not one that made her feel any more "alien" than she always had in Paris. "I'm bilingual—I think, speak, read, and write French as easily as I do English. When I ended up in high school in Philadelphia, the only place I felt even remotely at home was in French class, where I couldn't help being the star. But even the French teacher resented me, I think. I mean, doing well in French in high school was almost a cop-out—I already had the equivalent of a college education in the literature, and I could talk and write rings around my teacher. She used to give me special assignments, probably searching through her old grad school papers for 'hard' topics or books to report on, but everything she gave me was a breeze. I'd memorized more Baudelaire than she'd ever read. It was the one area of my life where I suppose I felt superior, but it didn't get me any brownie points, just more resentment. It just reinforced how weird everyone found me. I know I came across as a snob. I hated America and Americans, and I made no secret of it. I had no friends in high school—literally none. I'd come home to our apartment and wait for my mother to pass out from her daily dose of wine and do two things in secret: listen, with earphones, to classical music on the radio and steal sips out of my mother's wine bottles. Each of these activities seemed equally illicit. 'Music' equaled my hated father. 'Wine' equaled my pathetic mother. By the end of high school, I was a secret drunk and a secretly yearning wanna-be musician. I thought of killing myself a lot in those days. I was so horribly, horribly alone. Even more alone as I realized another truth about my secret desires: the only creatures in the world who held any appeal to me were women. I fixated on my French teacher mostly. She was only in her mid-twenties, not long out of grad school. She was beautiful—a blond out of Martha's Vineyard. As American as I could never be. I think I knew then that I hated Americans because I was so envious of their easy sense of being American. I envied anybody who had an identity they didn't question. I dreamed about this French teacher; I'd compose letters to her, really erotic letters, that I now see had a lot of details about sex my mother had told me when I was a little girl. Then I'd tear those letters up. God, I was so locked up. Locked up—and angry. The anger, it turned out, was my savior."

When Shane graduated from high school, she decided to move to Boston—alone. "I had a very specific mission. While I had no money for college, I'd investigated the music programs at the New England Conservatory and Boston Conservatory and figured out ways to audit certain classes. Some of the lecture courses I found I could just sneak into with no one being the wiser. I got part-time jobs as a 'domestic,' walking dogs for rich people who lived on Beacon Hill, cleaning apartments, baby-sitting bratty little kids, sometimes even tutoring them in French. I was exotic enough, I guess, that I quickly got a reputation as a sort of European 'au pair' girl—I was kind of trendy to employ, I think. I packed every off hour with music classes at various Boston schools but told none of my employers what I was doing—told nobody anything I was doing. There was only one person I cared about, anyway. Another blond woman, a lawyer. She'd recently gotten divorced and needed someone to clean her apartment, take care of her plants, walk her dog—and she became the center of my life. I fell totally completely in love with her. What clinched the deal was, she played the piano. She had a beautiful Steinway grand and, sometimes, when she got home early and overlapped with my time working in her apartment, would play Chopin. I would melt. All of the best part of France came back to me—she played so expressively, so beautifully, and with such amazing concentration. Sometimes she'd catch me staring at her when she played—and she'd smile. I could go for weeks on one of those smiles."

Shane says she couldn't go even for a night, however, without drinking. "It was controlled drinking at first. I mean, I'd buy two bottles of whatever good red wine I could find on sale and by morning they'd both be gone. I was so incredibly disciplined: I'm amazed when I think of how much I drank and how much I sort of *willed* myself into never having a hangover. Despite drinking almost as much as my mother drank, I was determined not to be the mess my mother was. I'd have my 'wine' and 'eat' it too. I didn't realize that the ability to drink huge quantities of alcohol and not be as outwardly affected by it as other people didn't single me out as a superior being—which is what I wanted to think—but as a fairly typical alcoholic. Alcoholics can go for years drinking everyone else under the table, which ironically makes them think they couldn't possibly be drunks. Anyway, the lids on the various parts of my life were screwed tight and, divided and compartmentalized as I was, I was somehow willing it all to work."

What about music? What were her aspirations here? "In a pawn shop, I found a viola. Brought up to hate my father and the violin, I in fact secretly loved the sound of it—of any stringed instrument. But I wanted something different, and I convinced myself that, just as I was a superior person when compared with my father and most of the rest of the human race (my lawyer employer the single exception—she was a goddess), so was the viola a superior instrument to the violin. The violin is a prima donna, always calling attention to itself, always hogging the mike. The darker, more secret viola was, however, the more profound and powerful of the two. When I was very young, my father actually taught me the fundamentals of bowing, fingering, how to hold the instrument, and so on. So I already had some idea of how to proceed. Then I picked a teacher, a grad student at New England Conservatory, whose hand-lettered three-by-five-inch card on a bulletin board announced that she was a *viola* teacher, not a violin-and-viola teacher like most of the rest of the teachers who advertised. Her come-on, 'Viola players of the world unite!' signaled to me that she was the sort of zealot I was looking for. Plus she wasn't charging much. So I hooked up with her, liked her enormously, liked her so much that she even began to nudge my blond lawyer pianist a bit off her pedestal. Now I had two blond women I was in love with. And I amazed both of them. The blond lawyer lady couldn't get over how meticulous I kept her apartment, all the extra touches I'd add, like bringing in flowers or polishing all of her cut-glass doodads in a display case. My blond viola teacher was simply astonished at my progress on the instrument. And so, sort of, was I. I mean, I was starting a stringed instrument as a nineteen-year-old—nobody imagines you can do that. But within a year, I was playing transcriptions of the Bach unaccompanied cello sonatas. I guess I kind of blew my teacher away. I wish I could say that I was thrilled with my own progress— I mean, rationally I knew I was doing something pretty incredible, but all I could think of was how much I still *couldn't* do. I was a terrible perfectionist, a taskmaster with myself. In fact, somehow the better I got, the more I hated myself. And the more I drank in secret. And the more my romantic fantasies about my teacher—who now had pretty much topped my lawyer pianist in my pantheon of goddesses—gnawed at me, made me feel even more lonely, more miserable than I had before."

And then came catastrophe. "I got a call from a weepy-sounding young man one morning," Shane says. "My viola teacher had just been killed—run over by one of Boston's crazy drivers. Just like that, she was gone. I spent the whole rest of that day sitting on my bed, dazed. The only thing I could think to do was drink. Because my discount liquor store had run a sale on Beaujolais Nouveau, I'd stocked up on six or so bottles of it. I went through one, then two, then three, and by the fourth was passed out on my bed. I woke up hours later and started in on the remaining bottles. My lawyer lady kept calling me—I'd never just not shown up before. Other employers called me for the same reason. But I was somewhere far away. I can't remember that time very well now. But I do know I got to the point where I was vomiting uncontrollably into my toilet. Somehow I didn't pass out, but wretching so violently did sort of sober me up a little—woke me up to begin to *feel* something again. What I felt was panic. I really felt, physically, like I was going to die—and I suddenly knew with all my heart and being that I didn't want to die. It was at that moment my recovery began."

Shane investigated options to get help. "I knew I needed help—it's funny; it's the one time in my life I knew I couldn't do something totally alone. I'd seen people walk in and out of the basement door to a church near my lawyer's home, seen the 'AA' sign on that door, and decided to walk there. I was afraid my employer might see me, so I wrapped myself in a turban and sunglasses and a big trench coat. I must have looked like a lunatic. It was fall, but unseasonably hot. If anything I probably drew more attention to myself! But I got to the church incognito and walked in on a meeting in progress. I sat down as if I had sneaked into some lecture class at the conservatory. It seemed vaguely illicit to be there. And I listened. I began to hear reflections of my own pain. I was amazed. For the first time in my life, I found people who were expressing at least some of the most secret fears and thoughts and jealousies and terrors I had felt. The idea hit that maybe I'd finally found someplace to 'belong.' It nearly knocked me off my chair."

Shane embraced AA with all the fervor she'd poured into her viola studies. "I got a sponsor right off, a middle-aged woman who seemed nice, who wouldn't nag at me." Shane pauses, looks down at the floor for a moment. "I told her my name was Jane. Not Shane. I wasn't willing, I guess, to let even this mild-seeming woman know my real name. I guess that's when I realized how *ashamed* I was of being me. I loved the order and simplicity and caring I found in AA, but I couldn't quite imagine being completely honest with anyone, not even a sponsor. There were things that were just—I don't know—too painful even for me to look at."

The nature of those "things" may seem surprising, Shane says. "I had a horror of telling anyone that I was a musician. On my own, I somehow got over my grief at losing my beloved viola teacher enough to hook up with another teacher, an elderly man who was as nonintimidating as my sponsor in AA. My drive to become a professional violist was so very strong—it's as if all the craving I once had for alcohol got channeled into music, again. But I didn't even let my sponsor know that I was a musician. The reasons will probably make you think I'm nuts. But I just projected this awful disapproval. 'You started the viola at nineteen? Well, I'm sure it's a nice hobby, but everyone knows that if you don't start an instrument early in childhood, you have no hope of becoming a virtuoso. And with no degree from a college or conservatory, well, you can't possibly expect to have a career in music.' I felt ashamed of my lack of formal education across the board, not just the lack of formal musical training. I read French literature like a demon, probably know more about Rimbaud and Verlaine than most doctoral students, but because I never went to college, I never let anyone know that I had this knowledge. It's like every single thing I could do well, I tried to hide, because I wasn't 'supposed' to be good at it; I hadn't had the conventional training to be good at it. So I instantly projected that everyone would think—would know—that I was a fake. I probably don't need to tell you that I never told my sponsor about something else 'shameful'—that I was lesbian. When I think of it, I never talked to my sponsor about anything important in my life at all!"

As far as "Jane's" sponsor knew, Shane's whole life revolved around her apartment-sitting and cleaning jobs. She shamefully hid her real passions from anyone she met in AA. "In the meantime, I was progressing leaps and bounds on the viola and in my 'stolen' musical education. I remember looking with horror at my teacher once when he said that the *Boston Herald* should really do a profile on me—how self-motivated I was, how I was becoming an expert instrumentalist without any of the usual background. It amazed me that he thought I should publicize what I felt I most had to hide! My lack of previous training seemed to him a virtue! I thought he was out of his mind or was just trying to be nice to me. I knew what the real world was like, I thought. I knew how they smirk at you, what they're really thinking behind your back." Shane shakes her head, still angry at her self-hate. "This secret musical, literary, and sexual me was the only 'me' that counted, and I was burying all of it whenever I wasn't in my viola teacher's living room. God, how I must have loathed myself!"

Burying the most central parts of her began to take some distressing tolls in her life. "I was committed to not drinking, one day at a time—and I truly didn't want to drink. But strange things began to happen. Once, back at my lawyer's apartment, watering her plants, I saw she'd left her wallet open on top of the piano. She'd come home early and was now on some long business phone call in her bedroom. Without even thinking, I opened the wallet, saw six twenty-dollar bills, and took two of them. I didn't question what I was doing for a moment. I remember getting home that night and finally registering that I'd stolen money from that client. The horror of it finally came crashing in—and a huge paranoia. Surely she'd suspect me! Would she call the police? Then the panic began to darken, turn slowly into anger. The woman had so much money, and I had so little. She really was a kind of snob—God knows what she *really* thought about me. Maybe she thought she was doing a good deed by employing a 'minority' housecleaner. What was I to her except some sort of vaguely pathetic exotic domestic? I began to hate her. I began, easily now, to rationalize my having taken the money. I think, secretly, I planned to do it again—not only with her, but with my other clients."

Shane cites other "strange" behavioral firsts. "I've always been skinny as a rail, but suddenly—I was working on a Brahms piece at the time—I started to eat more, craving stuff I'd never even liked when I was a kid. Cream-filled pastries. Fatty sausages. I began to gain weight. At first people told me I looked better since I'd been almost anorecticly thin before that. But then I started to get fat! I remember once passing a store window and getting a glimpse of this heavy woman lumbering by—and being shocked that it was me. I talked to my sponsor about this but quite honestly didn't know what to make of it. She suggested that the same need to escape my feelings I'd satisfied by drinking was hitting me in different ways. But I couldn't quite buy that. There was something about the impulse to eat—like the impulse to steal from my employers, and by now I'd become quite a deft thief not only at my lawyer's house but with the rest of my 'rich' clients—that was automatic. It was like I suddenly became unconscious. I had no 'feelings' at all. I wasn't aware of being scared or angry or depressed or sad or—anything. I just *wanted*. That was it. There was something almost animal-like about it. And then . . ." Shane trembles slightly at the memory. "Then I got caught. I mean really right-in-the-act nabbed. It was at my lawyer's house. Her wallet was on the piano, where it hadn't been for some weeks, which did make me wonder a little if she were catching on. But there it was again, open, and stuffed with more bills than I'd ever seen in it. She'd never miss the few bills I'd take. I felt this huge surge of delight, I think especially because her having left it there meant she didn't suspect me of anything, and I could go on stealing as long as I liked." The second Shane's hand was in the wallet, the lawyer walked in. "She said five words," Shane whispers. "'I thought so. Please leave.' That was it. I didn't even look at her. I just took my coat and left. By the time I was on the sidewalk, I nearly collapsed—it felt like my legs had no strength. I was once again in a complete state of shock. It dimly occurred to me that this might be a good time to call my sponsor but—good God, how could I ever tell her or anyone else what had just happened? So I did what I did the last time I'd been in shock. I made a beeline for the liquor store and stocked up on wine. I remember it was also Beaujolais Nouveau—a year had passed since the last binge, the one that ended in my quitting drinking. But now I had only one goal: to drink myself into oblivion, hopefully one from which I would not wake up."

Shane bought the wine, went home, sank onto her bed, and began to drink. About six hours and three bottles of wine later, the phone rang. "My sponsor's voice crackled onto the answering machine. 'Hi, Jane,' she said, 'Just wanted to check in. You there?' She waited; she knew I usually screened calls. I don't know what got into me. I picked the receiver up. I was absolutely blasted drunk and no longer able, as I once had been, to sound sober. I remember thinking as my first words slurred out how like my mother I suddenly sounded. 'I wanna die' is what I think I told her. I really don't remember. The only thing I can remember is that I felt the way I had when I'd grabbed for pastry or money—nothing. It was like an animal reflex, only this time the reflex told me to tell the truth. I must have told her I was drinking. All she said was, 'I'll be right over.' At least I think she said that. I think so because, within about twenty minutes, she'd arrived at my door."

Shane's sponsor arranged to get her into a Boston hospital rehab. "The lady's amazing," Shane says. "She didn't bat an eyelash, didn't lecture me, didn't do anything but take me to the hospital. I mean, she wasn't cold or anything; she was her old sweet warm helpful self. And when I got out—those two weeks are mostly a blur to me; all I can really remember is when I got out—there she was to pick me up. She took me to her apartment, not mine. I'd lost weight in the rehab, and there was some glimmer of the old svelte me. She complimented me on how I looked. We sat down in her kitchen, and she made and poured me a cup of herbal tea. Then she said, very simply, 'Now, why don't you start telling me the truth?'"

Shane's eyes grow tearful. "Tell the truth to someone? I realized in that instant that I had never ever—not once in my life— told anything like the 'whole truth' to anyone. My whole life, my whole self was a closely guarded secret. But I was so steamrolled, I was so vulnerable, and I guess I realized that I truly did trust this woman. Maybe even love her. So I started—it makes me laugh a little now; it's like something out of an old 1940s 'Drunk Sees the Light!' movie—I started by saying, 'My name is Shane. Not Jane. s-h-a-n-e. And I am one hell of a violist. And I am one basket case of an alcoholic.'"

Shane says she did the equivalent of a biographical Fourth Step and by the end of it, her sponsor was in tears. "I honestly didn't understand at first why she was crying. I finally asked her— it alarmed me. What was she seeing in my story that I didn't? As far as I was concerned, my story was of a screwed-up girl who lied and manipulated her way through life. What was heartwarming about that? If anything, I expected to be scolded for all the things I'd done—not cared for. But my sponsor tried to explain. 'You feel so alone,' is basically what she said. 'And it breaks my heart.'"

This turned into a life-changing moment, what Shane says was "the start of my real recovery. My impulse is to hide my 'lack of credentials'—and what I guess I realized when I saw my sponsor's sad caring response to my story is that I wanted to hide because I felt somehow *congenitally* inadequate. There was no real hope for me. I could try to compensate for the rest of my life— even get some degree at a college or conservatory—but it would never stamp out the fact that I was born a fake. Born missing some essential parts. I didn't realize then that this simply made

me like most other alcoholics in the world, feeling like irrepara-
bly damaged goods. But the lesbian part is what really got to me—
I mean, seeing that my sponsor did not react in horror when I told
her I was attracted to women. What she said was, 'That's wonderful. I did think you might be. And I've been trying to think of
an excuse to introduce you to a friend of mine I play bridge with.
She was married once until she couldn't stand living the lie—and
she's just come out. She's feeling pretty vulnerable. I always had
the idea you'd be a good person for her to talk to, because you
know how painful it is to hide. But I was always afraid you'd think
I was matchmaking, so I never brought it up.'"

Shane says, "You can't know how alien it was for me to sit and
talk like this, tell somebody not only one of my secrets, but all of
them—and then have that somebody respond with love and caring and empathy. It was like all my assumptions about human beings took a grenade in the gut. Maybe I didn't realize how much
help there was to be had. I'm still quaking from the idea that I
might not have to be so alone."

This transformative moment was only six months ago, and
Shane says, "I am a total fledgling baby bird. All I can do is open
my eyes wide, blink, and feed—not, thank God, anymore on pastries and Beaujolais Nouveau, but on the kind of help my sponsor is giving me. I met her friend and through that woman have
hooked up with a group of lesbians, some of whom are in recovery, one of whom is a professional French horn player. Sometimes
I can't believe how vast the world is and how much more of it is
welcoming me to enter it. I've now got friends, and they know all
the important facts about me. They get annoyed at me sometimes
when I start in on my 'I'll never be any good because I have no
credentials' shtick—sometimes they even get me to laugh at it. I
don't know. Maybe in time I'll get over this horrible feeling of in-
adequacy. But even if I don't entirely get over it, maybe I'll learn

to act in positive ways nonetheless." Shane smiles. "Actually, I did that already. My viola teacher has passed on some beginning students to me, whom I'm teaching privately. He said he couldn't imagine a better teacher for someone just starting out."

Does Shane see a connection between her urges to steal and overeat and the urge to drink? "I know the obvious answer— I mean, yes, of course there's a connection. All of those frantic pursuits helped me to flee whatever moment I was in that I could not tolerate. But you must understand that most of the time— even when I wasn't drunk, but was inhaling Napoleons or stealing—I simply didn't feel anything. It's like I know rationally that these other behaviors served a similar purpose to getting drunk, but the scary thing is that they sort of hit me from behind, took me over by surprise, and totally overwhelmed any will I might have had to resist them. It's the *irresistibility* that scares me. And it's that powerlessness I feel that's brought me so much more strongly back to AA, or at least to my sponsor's version of AA, which seems totally designed to help me accept that powerlessness, trust that if I stick to certain bedrock decisions, and—oh God, this still feels like the impossible part—take pains to repair what damage I can, I *will* be able to resist the next compulsive tidal wave. And what my sponsor means by 'repair' is to do the Eighth and Ninth Steps. Where you make amends. I know I've got to pay back the money I've stolen. I know that to get better, I've not only got to be honest about what I feel and do, but take certain actions that will connect me more strongly to the world. Thank God there's no time clock about this. I still feel so much shame. But I also feel so much hope." Shane smiles again. "And the worst part is, I'm always dragging my viola out to play for people. Would you like to hear some Bach?"

## The Wisdom to Know the Difference

Alcoholics and addicts know what it is to crave. The gay men and lesbian addicts and alcoholics you've met in these pages know something more, however: they know that their cravings are important. They do not see them pathologically, at least not as a first reflex. They may decide that some of the behaviors their cravings urge them to engage in may be in some ways "pathological"—or in Grace's phrase, "get in the way"—but the primal motive is one that rushes them toward pleasure, a solution to unbearable pain, a decision to choose life over death.

When Shane "relapsed" (went back to drinking), it was in the wake of having reacted to her cravings by reflex, of "grabbing" to steal or to eat before giving herself even the chance to understand what she was really grabbing for, which turns out—now that she *has* learned to reflect, now that she's less fearful about looking at her cravings—to be for something very much more fundamental than money or even food. "They're clear substitutes for love," Shane says. "And I realize now that I grabbed for anything that would fill the hole, the ache for love, inside me—grabbed in a knee-jerk way because I had buried too many feelings and thoughts for too long. It's like they backed up in a drain and just exploded into action—stealing, eating. *I had to be fed:* that was all my unconscious mind knew, I guess. But what I needed to be fed was acceptance and love and a feeling of safety. Money and food don't give me that any more than Beaujolais Nouveau ever did. It's not that now I've identified more clearly what it is I'm craving that I'm suddenly able to fulfill that craving—I mean, I'm still lonely and I still feel pain. But I know that satisfying this craving can't come from any substance or liquid or material thing. Satisfying it has to begin with *willingness*—willingness to look inside myself and share what I find. There are people in my life now who reinforce this understanding. I think, if I'm able to keep my pact to be with them and talk to them every day, I'll be able to keep my pact not to deaden myself in the old ways. And it's not nothing that I want you to hear me play the viola. My viola has things to say too, things I don't know how to say in any other way. Which is maybe why I want to play it more for people. Like it or not, I'm gonna let it all out. The biggest miracle in my life is that I'm able to say—and mean—that."

Perhaps I've struck the note enough, but Shane makes it ring sonorously (this time in the smoky alto tones of a viola) again: our cravings bring us, ultimately, to an incredibly nourishing encounter with *who we really are*. They are a guide, not a disease. And the way we can learn to use them as a guide is, first, to learn to tolerate them without bolting away—or getting high or drunk. So much of any successful approach to recovery you've read about here brings us back to that old word *analysis*. *You've got to open your eyes*.

How to get to a point of willingness—of receptivity—where you can conceive of keeping your eyes open: this is where we ram into the mystery, the miracle of change. However, we can always choose to be more honest, with ourselves and with people we know we can trust, about what's going on inside us, no matter what the degree of that willingness and receptivity. In fact, we hold our "truths" back at our peril. The unconscious quality of Shane's stealing and overeating are flags that *cravings will out*— either in conscious ways over which we have some kind of control or in unconscious ways that hit us like a piece of falling concrete.

The Serenity Prayer—"God grant me the serenity to accept the things I cannot change, the courage to change the things I can, and the wisdom to know the difference"—gives us a clue about the kind of action we may be able to take. Perhaps number one in the "courage to change the things I can" category is something like "Be honest." Tell the truth—to somebody. To yourself. Say the words you're thinking but until now thought you could never speak. They are what will make you "free" and, eventually, allow you the power to keep from killing yourself with a drug or a drink. They are also words that will help you to accept who you are—as a gay man, lesbian, Radical Faerie, or violist.

"Coming out" isn't possible until we've gone in and know what we want to "come out" with. If the women and men in this book are any indication, you'll find more than you dreamed existed when you take that interior journey yourself—sober.

# About the Author

Guy Kettelhack is the author and coauthor of more than twenty-five nonfiction books, including *Easing the Ache*, *Dancing around the Volcano*, *Sober and Free*, *The Wit and Wisdom of Quentin Crisp*, *First-Year Sobriety*, *Second-Year Sobriety*, and *Third-Year Sobriety*. A graduate of Middlebury College, Kettelhack has done post-graduate work in English literature at the Bread Loaf School of English in Vermont and Lincoln College at Oxford University, and he has pursued coursework in psychoanalysis at the Centers for Modern Psychoanalytic Studies in New York and Boston. He lives in New York City.